Women
WHO MADE A
Difference

Life Lessons from Women of the Bible

MARTHA TYLER

Regular Baptist Press
1300 North Meacham Road
Schaumburg, Illinois 60173-4806

WOMEN WHO MADE A DIFFERENCE: LIFE LESSONS FROM WOMEN
OF THE BIBLE
© 2002
Regular Baptist Press • Schaumburg, Illinois
1-800-727-4440
www.regularbaptistpress.org

Printed in U.S.A.
All rights reserved
RBP5271 • ISBN: 0-87227-745-3

Third printing— 2004

Contents

Dedication

• To the memory of my husband, Don, who was the most loving and encouraging man I know. He was a constant source of inspiration and information.

• To my two daughters, Debra McMillan and Joanna Kubiak, two women who have truly made a difference.

• To my good friend Callie Butler and my son-in-law Gene McMillan who helped me in my many computer struggles.

• To my dear friend Doris Tabler, who helped me so much by reading many of these lessons and giving me her input.

Preface

CAN ONE WOMAN make a difference? I believe so! The ten lessons in this study present twelve Bible women who did just that. They were women of various ages, from different backgrounds and social levels. Some were career women who were used of God in national leadership; some were stay-at-home moms who focused on their homes and families. Most were Jewish women, but two were Gentiles. From the woman who brought sin into the world to the one who brought our Savior into the world, all were women who made a difference.

Even though you may be familiar with these Bible characters, I trust you will benefit in the following ways: (1) gain new knowledge and insights about these women; (2) be encouraged to become all that God intends for you to be; (3) determine to serve God better than you ever have before.

Each lesson starts with an overview of the character's life. Then the lesson moves into "Study the Scriptures." The subheads in this section will make it easy to spread your Bible study over several days, if you so desire. The final section of each lesson is "Make a Difference in Your World." As you reflect on the things you have learned about each Bible woman, you will want to make some definite decisions and take some deliberate actions to put the truth into practice.

So pick up your Bible and a pencil, ask God to open your heart to His truth, and study each lesson with the determination to apply the truth to your life.

And remember . . .

Never underestimate the power of a woman!

Eve: First Lady of Creation

Genesis 1—3

EVE WAS THE FIRST lady of creation and the mother of us all. She was the *first* woman, the *first* wife, and the *first* mother. She had no role models or examples. She had no one to tell her how to do things. She had neither mother nor mother-in-law. Except for one notorious deed, very little is known about this first lady of creation. But this one deed gave Eve the distinction of making the *greatest difference* of any woman who ever lived. Her action still affects us today—and, sad to say, not for good.

Eve lived in Paradise with a husband who adored her. She was beautiful and intelligent and had the perfect marriage. She was the one woman who could honestly say that she had nothing to wear!

At the time of her creation, Eve was innocent. She had never sinned. She and her husband had perfect fellowship with God.

Adam and Eve were blessed by God. He put them in charge of His wonderful creation. They were to rule over it. But things changed in Paradise.

Satan used a serpent as his instrument to get to Eve. He tempted her and cast doubt on what God had said. He changed the meaning of what God had said by *ever so slightly* changing the wording. Satan tried to create an image of God as someone who was withholding something wonderful from her. Satan

succeeded. Eve took of the fruit and gave some to her husband, thus ending the only perfect marriage in history.

Creation was marred, and sickness, disease, death, and all evil were introduced into the world. Every person since Adam and Eve has been born a sinner.

Yet God still loved Adam and Eve. He sought them and made a way to restore fellowship. Eve's life shows us how God deals with us when we sin and how our fellowship with Him can be restored.

Study the Scriptures

Life in a Perfect Environment

Let's look at life in the Garden of Eden. God created the heavens and the earth plus all the plants and animals; then He created mankind. The creation of people was special and different than the rest of creation. The animals were created in pairs, male and female. But God made only Adam at first; later He made Eve. Someone has jokingly said that God must have taken a good look at Adam and said, "I can do better than that!" so He made Eve.

1. Each time God finished a day of creation, He looked at it and said it was good. But after creating Adam, what did God say? Read Genesis 2:18.

2. God put a need in Adam's heart. Then God met Adam's need. How did He do this? Read Genesis 2:18 again.

God gave Adam time to name the animals before He made Eve. (Wouldn't you like to know what language Adam spoke as he named the animals?) The animals must have passed by two

by two because Adam realized a big difference between himself and the animals.

3. How did naming the animals show Adam his need for a mate? Read Genesis 2:19 and 20.

Adam noticed that Mr. Lion had Mrs. Lion and Mr. Elephant had Mrs. Elephant, but Mr. Adam had no Mrs. Adam.

4. God allowed time for Adam to realize he was incomplete. Why do you think God did this?

5. Read Genesis 2:21 and 22. Describe how God made Eve.

Someone has said that God did not take the bone from Adam's head so that he could boss Eve, nor from his feet so he could walk on her. God took the bone from under Adam's arm so he could protect Eve and from close to his heart so he would love her.

Wouldn't you like to have seen the look on Adam's face when he saw Eve?

6. Did Adam recognize Eve as the mate God had created for him (Genesis 2:23)?

Eve had just come from God's hand, and Adam recognized immediately that she was what he needed to fill the vacuum in his

life. He was grateful. This is a good lesson for a married woman: Be thankful for your mate and recognize him as God's gift.

God designed Eve to help Adam. She was a helper who was "meet," or suitable, for him (Genesis 2:18). Some women think being a helper is degrading. Other women seem to think their role is to be just like a man. Neither is true. As hard as some women try, they still cannot be exactly like men. Why? The Creator designed them to be different—"male and female created he them" (Genesis 1:27). Notice that "different" does not mean "inferior."

Women find fulfillment when they function as God designed them. Adam could not make it through the first twenty-four hours without a helper. The role of helper is a good role. The Bible says that God is our helper (Hebrews 13:6). By nature, women seem to be good helpers to their husbands, children, aged parents, and even their bosses. God made Adam to take care of the ground and Eve to take care of Adam.

A Look at the Perfect Couple

7. Adam and Eve were no doubt beautiful beyond description, with healthy bodies and great personalities. What pattern (image, or likeness) did God use to make mankind? Read Genesis 1:26.

This does not mean that we look like God physically, but that we possess the characteristics of God, such as an intellect, emotion, and will.

8. What does the first phrase of Genesis 1:28 say that God did?

What a wonderful privilege Adam and Eve had to be made by God and then to be blessed by Him!

Genesis 2:7 summarizes God's creation of mankind. God made us with self-consciousness, self-determination, and the ability to choose between right and wrong. We can feel complex emotions such as joy or sadness. We can speak intelligently—

not just parrot what someone taught us to say. We have the ability for complex thoughts such as math and science. But most of all, we can worship and fellowship with God.

At first things went well for Eve. She enjoyed intimacy with her husband and with God. But calamity lay ahead as the *serpent* entered this story. As we look at Eve's temptation, may God help us to learn principles that will help us in our times of temptation.

Temptation and How It Works

Did snakes talk in the Garden of Eden? I do not know. But I know that Satan spoke through *this* snake. It was the instrument he used to get to Eve. Eve did not seem at all surprised that a snake talked. It seems that before sin entered the world, snakes were beautiful and intelligent creatures. Adam and Eve may have spent a good deal of time around snakes. At any rate, Eve easily entered into a discussion with this creature.

Satan knew of the fellowship between God and Adam and Eve. And Satan saw the tender love between Adam and Eve. Satan was bent on destroying these relationships. Satan still hates the children of God and wants to destroy these wonderful things (e.g., relationships, love, fellowship) in their lives.

9. How does 1 Peter 5:8 describe the Devil and his activities?

If you knew that someone was prowling around and trying to kill you, wouldn't you be on the lookout for him? Since the Bible tells us that Satan is out to devour us, shouldn't we be on the lookout for him?

Satan came to Eve as a friend, appearing to be something he was not. He offered Eve a way to have happiness and wisdom. He was deceitful and didn't tell the whole truth. He is still doing these same things today.

10. How did Satan undermine God's Word? Read Genesis 3:1.

Unbelief starts with questioning what God says. Shading God's truth, even if it is only a little, can be disastrous.

At first glance, Eve appeared to repeat what God had said. But as we look more closely, we see she was actually tampering with God's Word.

11. What did Eve add to God's Word? Compare Genesis 3:3 with Genesis 2:16 and 17.

This addition may have seemed logical to Eve, but it was *not* what God had said. We need to be careful that we do not add to (or subtract from) God's Word—even if we think it is logical.

12. What *did* God say about eating fruit from the trees in the Garden (Genesis 2:16, 17)?

Let's look at the sequence of Eve's sin.

• She listened to Satan. She let him express his ideas to her. She started thinking that maybe God was wrong, that maybe she was capable of deciding good from bad herself.

• She and the serpent looked at the fruit together. The Bible says to flee temptation. (See, for instance, 2 Timothy 2:22.) We are to distance ourselves from sin, not see how close we can get without sinning.

• She lusted and desired the fruit that would make her wise. She thought this fruit would make her happy. It looked good. What a giant step in the wrong direction! From that time to the present, all evils are the result of this act of lustful disobedience. Still today we are guilty of demanding immediate gratification, of not considering the effect of our actions on our future.

• Eve took the fruit and ate it. The previous three steps led to the actual sin.

• She shared it with her husband. When we sin, we often

involve others. Women have a tremendous power to influence their families for right or wrong.

13. Dealing with temptation is an age-old problem. Read James 4:7. What two commands are given in this verse and what is the result of obeying these commands?

14. How will obeying these commands help us deal with temptation?

The High Cost of Sin

15. What do these New Testament verses say about Eve's temptation: 2 Corinthians 11:3 and 1 Timothy 2:14?

Satan tricked Eve into doubting God's Word. Strangely enough, he uses the same tactics today. We know how he operates, yet we just keep buying his line!

16. Temptation comes into our lives in what three ways according to 1 John 2:16?

Eve opened herself to sin by gazing upon the forbidden fruit. She saw that it was good for food ("the lust of the flesh") and

pleasant to the eye ("the lust of the eyes") and that it would make her wise ("the pride of life"), so she took it and ate it.

17. Notice the setting in Genesis 3:12–17 as God met with the serpent, Eve, and Adam. Where does it appear that Adam was when Eve was tempted?

Adam did not try to stop Eve from eating; he ate also. He was as guilty as she was.

18. What happened as soon as Adam and Eve ate the forbidden fruit (Genesis 3:7, 8)?

When they committed the fatal deed, the promised results came (though not as they had hoped). Adam and Eve tried to hide from their sin and cover it. They lost the bliss of their innocence. They gained, instead, a sense of guilt and shame. Before they sinned, they knew good and did it. After they sinned, they still knew good, but they could not do it. Before they sinned, they were ignorant of evil and did not do it. After they sinned, they knew evil but could not stop doing it. (This condition is described in Romans 7:19.) Adam and Eve were defiled; they had become sinners.

Adam and Eve realized they were naked, so they sewed fig leaves together for clothes. This was an attempt to cover their sin by the works of their hands. Yet in their hearts they knew that their works were not good enough, so they tried to hide from God. As their children, we tend to do the same thing.

19. What does Isaiah 64:6 say our righteousnesses are like?

20. How can we be saved from our sin? Read Ephesians 2:8 and 9.

As soon as Adam and Eve ate of the forbidden fruit, they died spiritually; that is, they were separated from God. In addition, they had started the process of physical death. God could have left Adam and Eve in their sin and never spoken to them again, but He didn't.

21. According to Genesis 3:9, what did God do?

God, in His mercy and grace, reached out to Adam and Eve. He is the same today; He reaches out to you and me (Psalm 103:10–14).

22. When God confronted Adam and Eve, the blame game began. Read Genesis 3:10–13. (a) Who did Adam blame?

    (b) Who did Eve blame?

By blaming Eve, Adam indirectly blamed God for giving him this woman. (Originally he was thrilled with her.) Eve blamed the serpent for deceiving her. We still tend to blame others for our sins instead of taking responsibility for our actions, don't we?

God killed an animal and used its skin to clothe Adam and Eve. This animal sacrifice pointed to the time Christ would die on the cross for your sins and mine. Have you accepted Jesus Christ as your Savior? Do you have a personal relationship with God? If you have never asked Jesus to be your Savior or are unsure whether you have, I invite you to read the following verses that clearly explain the plan of salvation.
- Romans 3:23—All have sinned.
- Romans 5:8—Christ died for our sins.
- Romans 6:23—God offers salvation as a free gift.
- John 1:12—Receive, by faith, God's free gift.

You may want to express your decision to God in prayer.

You could pray something like this: "Dear God, I know I am a sinner. I believe Jesus died for my sin. I personally and willingly ask You to save me. Help me live for You. In Jesus name, amen."

The story of Eve was not given as a matter of history, but to instruct us and to help us in our own lives. We learn from Eve how NOT to deal with temptation. As we gain victory in these areas, we can make a difference in our world.

Make a Difference in Your World

1. We all face temptation; even Jesus was tempted. It is not a sin to be tempted, but it is a sin to yield to temptation. If you feel you are being tempted in a certain area, follow the example of Christ in Matthew 4:1–11. Resist temptation by claiming the promises of God.

2. We learn from Eve that it is best to stay away from temptation. Pause and take a look at your life. What specific temptations do you face? Do you try to stay away from these temptations, or do you see how close you can get to them without yielding? Memorize James 4:7 and obey the commands of that verse.

3. When Adam and Eve sinned, God sought them and made a way to restore fellowship with them again. Regardless of what type of sin is in your life, God loves you and longs to have fellowship with you. Read 1 John 1:9. Confess your sin and accept His forgiveness today.

4. What lessons have you learned from Eve that will help you make a difference in your world?

Sarah: A Woman of Faith

Genesis 12—23

YOU'VE PROBABLY HEARD the saying, "Behind every great man is a great woman." Sarah was just that! More is said about her than any other woman in Scripture. Sarah was a woman who truly made a difference! Through her came the prophets, the Bible, and, yes, even our Savior! That makes her a pretty important lady!

Sarah was a beautiful woman whose name meant "princess." Sarah, like her husband, Abraham, is listed in Hebrews 11 as an example of one who excelled in faith. God called Sarah to leave her country, her family, and all that she knew and held dear to go to a new country and establish a new people. She obeyed—not knowing *why* she had to go *where* she was to go, *when* she would get there, or *how* God would fulfill His promise. Although her faith faltered at times, most of her life shows great faith in God.

Moving was a common event in Sarah's life as she followed her husband from one place to another. The one thing she longed for above all else was a son, and God, in His goodness, gave her one when she was old enough to be a great, great grandmother. Eventually her descendants became as numerous as the stars in the sky.

❀ ❀ ❀

Study the Scriptures

Moving On

The story of Sarah begins in Genesis 12. God gave Abram (later called Abraham), Sarah's husband, a special call.

1. What did God tell Abraham to do? Read Genesis 12:1.

2. What did God promise Abraham? Read Genesis 12:2 and 3.

3. What did Abraham do (Genesis 12:4, 5)?

At an age when most women are grandmothers, Sarah gave up a life of luxury to follow her husband to a different land, where, as God had said, Abraham would become a great nation—an amazing promise since the couple was childless! They didn't know where God was sending them, but they obeyed and packed up their belongings and moved. And they kept moving on and on (probably about a thousand miles). During this time Sarah may have set up "tent keeping" at least a dozen times, and she was no spring chicken!

Modern-day employment often causes families to relocate. It can be difficult to leave family, friends, church, and schools. Just remember your family roots are not in a *place* but in a *person*—Jesus Christ. He can help you adjust and can delight you with wonderful plans and promises for your future, just as He did for Sarah.

4. Sarah's life is mentioned in 1 Peter 3:1–6 as an example of the right kind of wife. In what way is Sarah's life an example for us to follow?

After Abraham and Sarah arrived in the land of Canaan, they encountered a famine. So they decided to go to Egypt.

5. Read Genesis 12:11–13. What did Abraham ask Sarah to do?

Although Sarah was Abraham's half sister (see Genesis 20:12), Abraham was lying. Sarah was his wife! Abraham may have thought that calling her his sister was not too bad since it was partially true, but in the eyes of God it was a lie.

6. How did this lie wrong Sarah (Genesis 12:15)?

The Egyptian princes saw Sarah, disguised as Abraham's beautiful sister, and recommended that Pharaoh add her to his harem. Pharaoh did just that!

7. How did God protect Sarah (Genesis 12:17–20)?

Even though a woman's husband is to be her protector, she needs to depend on God for protection more than on her husband.

Husbands are human and sometimes fail; God never fails. God honored Sarah's submissive heart and supernaturally protected her.

Still Sarah's heart was unsettled because she was barren. God had promised to make Abraham a great nation, but the couple had no children. Any woman who has wanted children but has been unable to conceive can surely understand Sarah's feelings. No cry echoes as deeply as that of a barren woman (Proverbs 30:15, 16).

Lapse of Faith

It had been about ten years since Abraham and Sarah had heard from God. They were getting impatient for God's fulfillment of His promise. Sarah may have rationalized that God had not specifically said that she, Sarah, was to be the mother of a child. Sarah tried to help God by human means.

Before you are too hard on Sarah, ask yourself how many times you have become impatient with God and have tried to work things out yourself.

Sarah loved Abraham and desperately wanted to fulfill his heart's desire. She was no doubt aware of what happened when Abraham asked God if Eliezer, his servant, could be the heir (Genesis 15:2, 3). The heir was to come from Abraham's own house (v. 4).

Sarah had given up hope that she could have a child, so she came up with a plan. Sarah may have had good motives, but she went about a good thing in a wrong way.

8. What did Sarah suggest to Abraham (Genesis 16:2)?

9. What was Hagar's nationality (Genesis 16:3)?

Perhaps Hagar joined Abraham and Sarah when they went to Egypt for a sojourn (a trip that was out of God's will). When

we stray from God's will, we often pick up something or someone that will later cause problems.

Sarah's plan was not a brand-new idea. Back in Ur, it was a common practice to use a maid as a surrogate mother. The problem was that this was not God's design! We, too, need to be careful that we do not accept the world's ideas for God's ideas.

10. According to Genesis 16:1 and 2, what three things contributed to Abraham's committing this sin?

Sarah had allowed a seed of doubt in her life to grow into a tree of unbelief. Doubt was understandable in her situation. She was too old to have a child. No woman—even in Sarah's day—had children at her age. She decided God needed help. Don't we often do the same thing? Oh, we rationalize this thing or that, but the real culprit is our lack of faith.

11. Unbelief is contagious. Sarah's doubt began affecting those around her. Have you ever gone through a trial of faith and had someone express doubt or unbelief to you? How did that make you feel? What did you wish the person had said instead? What did you learn about helping others who are going through trials of faith?

12. Does God sit in Heaven and try to think of ways to make life difficult for us? No! He loves us and wants the best for us. How does Matthew 7:11 describe God's attitude toward us?

Sarah's Plan Backfires

13. In a community of tents there were no secrets. Soon the whole compound knew Hagar and Abraham were having a child. Hagar's attitude began to change toward Sarah. How did Hagar feel toward her boss? Read Genesis 16:4.

Hagar began to see herself in a more prominent position and flaunted her pregnancy. *She* was having Abraham's child. As Sarah watched Hagar's belly swell with life, she may have suspected that Hagar thought she was entitled to some of Abraham's wealth too.

Sarah regretted ever suggesting this idea and complained to Abraham. Since Sarah had masterminded the whole idea to begin with, he told her to do whatever she pleased to Hagar. Sarah dealt with Hagar so harshly that she ran for her life.

Hagar sat alone in the wilderness confused, frightened, and betrayed. It was in this pregnant single mother's hour of need that the angel of the Lord came to Hagar with a special message.

14. Where did the angel tell her to go and what was she to do? Read Genesis 16:9.

15. What did he say about the future of this child (Genesis 16:10)?

16. What was Hagar to name her child, and what would he be like (Genesis 16:11, 12)?

Imagine having a child like this in your home! Instead of the

blessing Sarah had envisioned, this child brought hatred and jealousy into her home. Eventually Abraham sent both Hagar and Ishmael away (Genesis 21:9–21).

17. Sarah's proposal ended up wronging many people. In what way(s) were each of the following people affected?
Abraham

Hagar

Sarah

Ishmael

Isaac

God's Promise Fulfilled

Thirteen more years passed with no word from God. Abraham and Sarah were only getting older. Humanly speaking, the birth of a child was impossible. God waited until no one could doubt that the birth of the promised son was directly of God.

18. What message from God did three men bring to Abraham? Read Genesis 18:10.

19. How did Sarah hear the news, and what was her response (Genesis 18:10, 12)?

This time God not only promised a child, but also gave a time when he would be born. At first Sarah laughed at what she heard. They were two old people, too old to produce a child.

20. We have a loving God Who knows our hearts and wants the best for us. What thought-provoking question did God ask in Genesis 18:14?

What a good question to ask ourselves as we face life's problems! If we focus on our problems, we become over-whelmed; but when we focus on God's great power, we have hope and joy for the future.

21. Even in her disbelief, Sarah *did* have faith. She was like the man in Mark 9:24. What did he say, and how can we apply these words to Sarah's situation?

22. What does Hebrews 11:1 say about faith?

23. Can we please God without faith? Why? Read Hebrews 11:6.

24. What does Hebrews 11:11 say about Sarah's faith?

Sarah did not lean on Abraham's faith. She had her own faith. Each person must have his or her own relationship with God. You cannot lean on your husband, parents, or pastor; you must have your own personal relationship with God.

Faith requires action. Sarah and Abraham had to take action on what God had said. They had to believe that what God had said would really happen and then to act accordingly.

God fulfilled His promise to Abraham and Sarah, and Isaac was born. His name meant "laughter."

25. Why was Isaac an appropriate name for this child? Compare Genesis 18:12 with Genesis 21:6.

Sarah's laughter of unbelief was turned to the laughter of joy and delight. She was reminded of this fact every time she spoke her son's name.

God gave Sarah thirty-seven more years to watch Isaac grow up and see God's blessing on him. She lived to be 127 years old! In spite of her lapses of faith, we remember Sarah as a woman of great faith, a woman who made a difference.

Make a Difference in Your World

1. Learning to rely on God to supply our needs is easier said than done. It requires faith. In Sarah we see a woman who vacillated between having great faith and relying on human resources. She went from finagling a way to make God's

promise come true to complete trust in His Word. We see the blessings of great faith and the consequences of relying on ourselves. Do you look at Sarah and say, "Been there, done that?" Which way are you presently living—by faith or by human resources?

2. Do you have situations in your life right now where God's Word is saying one thing and circumstances the other? Follow God's counsel in Philippians 4:6 and 7: "Be careful for nothing; but in every thing by prayer and supplication with thanksgiving let your requests be made known unto God. And the peace of God, which passeth all understanding, shall keep your hearts and minds through Christ Jesus." Apply these verses to your own situation.

3. Being a woman of faith at some point in the past does not guarantee victory today. Each day you must trust God to help you meet the challenges you face. You cannot be victorious today on yesterday's faith. Think of a situation where you need to act in faith today and do it.

4. Sarah's life also teaches us that when we fail, we have a God Who will forgive. First John 1:9 is still true today. Confess your sin to Him.

5. What lessons have you learned from Sarah that will help you make a difference in your world?

Rebekah: The High Cost of Scheming

Genesis 24; 26:1—28:9

REBEKAH'S LIFE reads like a romantic novel. One day a man appeared at the well where she watered her family's flocks. This man wanted her to become the bride of his wealthy master's son. She was no doubt very impressed. She was even more impressed when he gave her and her family beautiful and expensive gifts. Rebekah must have thought, "It can't get much better than this." He asked her to leave immediately, and, without hesitation, she did.

The marriage seemed to get off to a good start. The Bible says that Isaac loved Rebekah. But her life was full of crisis situations and conflict. Even before their birth, her children were at odds with each other. Plus each parent had a favorite child.

As time passed, Isaac's love for Rebekah seemed to weaken. He did not want to die for his beautiful wife, so he passed her off as his sister. This action on Isaac's part left Rebekah exposed to grave danger. No doubt Rebekah was hurt and wounded. Perhaps that is why she used her knowledge of trickery on Isaac. Her conniving seemed to work, and her favorite son got the blessing. However, deceit is never of God.

In spite of all her shenanigans, Rebekah was a woman who made a difference, and we can learn from her.

❀ ❀ ❀

Study the Scriptures

"I Will Go"

1. What do the following verses tell us about Rebekah?
Genesis 24:15, 16

Genesis 24:45, 46

Genesis 24:56–58 (especially verse 58)

It was no coincidence that Abraham's servant met Rebekah. He prayed for direction, and she fit all the qualifications for which he was looking. She was an answer to prayer.

When Abraham's servant asked for a drink, she fetched water not only for him but also for his thirsty camels. She did this quickly and ran to the well for more water. She was energetic and found joy in serving others. When you are called upon to serve your family, your heart attitude is exposed. Do you serve eagerly with joy and enthusiasm?

Rebekah had an interesting family background. She grew up in Mesopotamia near the city of Nahor. Rebekah's grandfather Nahor was Abraham's brother, which made Isaac and Rebekah fairly close relatives. Rebekah's most notable relative was Laban, her brother, who seemed to be the head of the family clan.

Rebekah had a sudden, radical change of plans. Just the day

before, she had no idea she would be moving to a different country and getting married; but she believed this plan was of God, so she answered, "I will go." What do you do when God brings unexpected circumstances into your life? Do you face them fearlessly, determined to follow God's leading? Or do you cling to your own plans, resenting the changes?

Rebekah was adventuresome. She willingly left the security of her home and her family to journey with a man she had met only a few hours ago to marry a man she had never met at all.

Let's look at her husband. Isaac was certainly a lot different than his father, Abraham. Isaac was passive rather than aggressive. When Isaac was forty, Abraham decided it was time to find a wife for his son. He sent his servant back to his homeland to find a suitable bride. The servant returned with Rebekah. Like most husbands and wives, Isaac and Rebekah were quite different.

2. What would make you think Isaac may have been a quiet, deep thinker? Read Genesis 24:63.

3. What would make you think Rebekah was a warm, outgoing type of person? Read Genesis 24:64 and 65.

Differences that attract at first can later repel. This change seems to have happened in Isaac and Rebekah's marriage.

4. Rebekah's marriage to Isaac was quite simple for such a wealthy family. (Once again we see Isaac's quiet nature with no desire for great fanfare.) How does Genesis 24:67 describe the marriage?

The sequence is interesting: Isaac took Rebekah into his mother's tent, and she became his wife; then Isaac loved her.

What's Happening Here?

5. Read Genesis 25:21. What problem did Rebekah face?

6. Compare Genesis 25:20 with 25:26 to find out how many years Isaac and Rebekah were married before they had children.

Where do you go when you can't figure out what's happening? In the midst of a trial, we sometimes forget God is with us. We *think* it is easier to go to people that we can see and touch. However, God knows our problems completely, while others know only what we tell them.

Infertility can be a heart-breaking problem, and Rebekah experienced this situation for many years. Isaac prayed to God, Who is the giver of life, for a child. Finally God answered, and Rebekah was pregnant.

Soon Rebekah faced another problem. She had so wanted a child, but something was definitely wrong in this pregnancy. She turned to God.

7. When she inquired of the Lord, what did He tell her? Read Genesis 25:23.

No wonder she felt so much movement! (See Genesis 25:22.)

8. Read Genesis 25:24–26 and describe the birth of the twins.

Jacob held Esau's heel as though trying to pull him back into the womb so that Jacob could be the firstborn. (The fight, which began at birth, continued for life!) Esau was so hairy that later Rebekah used the skin of a goat as a substitute for Esau's hand. Can you imagine someone that hairy? Jacob was smooth skinned.

9. What does Genesis 25:27 say about Rebekah's twin sons?

If you have more than one child in your family, you know each child is different. Have you ever marveled how two children with the same parents and same environment can grow up to be so very different?

Playing Favorites

10. Rebekah and Isaac made a huge mistake in bringing up their boys. This mistake is probably one of the worse mistakes a parent can make. What was it? Read Genesis 25:28.

Favoritism causes terrible problems in a home. It makes children compete with each other. These boys did not need to be encouraged to compete since they started fighting before birth. Tragically, this trait was passed on to the next generation. Jacob had a favorite son, Joseph. Jacob gave Joseph a beautiful coat to show his favoritism; as a result, Joseph's brothers hated him. Ephesians 6:4 tells fathers not to provoke their children to wrath. Favoritism provokes a child.

Sometimes parents show favoritism without realizing it. They may blame one child for everything that goes wrong, while the other child is never at fault. Or a parent may say, "Now *this* child is a handful," implying that another child is not.

Sometimes children think parents favor one sibling more than another when it isn't true; but, unfortunately, many times it is true. All children cannot be treated the same. However, each child in a family should be treated with *love* and *dignity.*

11. Why did Isaac love Esau? Read Genesis 25:28.

12. Why did Rebekah love Jacob? Read Genesis 25:27-29.

Rebekah's marriage took a turn for the worse when a famine came and Isaac decided to pack up and journey into the Philistines' camp. God appeared to Isaac and told him not to go to Egypt. (Isaac was probably headed there eventually.) Instead of going to Egypt, Isaac dwelt at Gerar (Genesis 26:6). Rebekah was somewhere between 60 and 100, but she was still incredibly beautiful. An old family failure reappeared.

13. What was it? Read Genesis 26:7.

Isaac told the same lie his dad had told. Abraham's lie was half true; Sarah was his half sister. Isaac's lie was entirely false. How often our children pick up on our weak spots and follow us more deeply into sin!

14. Why did Isaac lie? Read Genesis 26:7 and 9.

15. How did Abimelech know Isaac lied? Read Genesis 26:8. (Note: This is not the same Abimelech that Abraham dealt with. Abimelech may have been a name for a king in that country.)

16. How did Isaac endanger Rebekah (Genesis 26:10)?

17. Isaac did not treat Rebekah the way God intended a husband to treat his wife. How does God say husbands are to treat their wives? Read Ephesians 5:25.

Isaac looked out for himself instead of his wife, leaving her to feel unloved and unprotected. He was willing for her to be degraded to protect himself. Genesis 26:10 indicates Rebekah would have been safe if the people knew she was married but in great danger if they thought she was single and available.

Disappointment in the Family

18. After forty years Rebekah become a mother-in-law. Whom did Esau marry? Read Genesis 26:34.

19. What nationality were Esau's wives (Genesis 26:34)?

20. How did Isaac and Rebekah feel about Esau's marriages to Canaanite women (Genesis 26:35)?

21. What was Esau's response when he saw that his parents were displeased with the women he had married? Read Genesis 28:8 and 9.

Apparently Esau didn't know he was *not* to marry a Canaanite woman. When Jacob was sent away to find a wife, Esau must have said to himself, "Is that what Mom and Dad were so mad about? Now I'll marry someone who pleases them." Isaac and Rebekah had not taught their children that it was wrong to marry an unbeliever. Don't miss this teaching for your children. What is the best way to keep from marrying an unbeliever? Never date one!

Rebekah's marriage had deteriorated to the point that there was little or no communication. Isaac did not call Rebekah to his bedside and say, "Honey, I think it is time for me to give my patriarchal blessing." Genesis 27:1–5 seems to indicate Isaac was trying to hide what he was going to do by asking for a special stew. The stew had nothing to do with the blessing; it was a decoy.

But Rebekah was too smart for Isaac. She had found out a lot of things by eavesdropping. She may have set up a network of spies in her household to carry information back to her.

A Tangled Web

22. What could Rebekah have done when Isaac tried to sneak behind her back and bless Esau?

23. As Isaac and Rebekah's conflict grew, no doubt they said words to each other that should not have been said. Let's look at what God says about our speech. Read Ephesians 4:29.

    (a) What are we not to let come out of our mouths?

    (b) What should come out of our mouths?

    (c) What will this kind of speech accomplish?

24. Read Ephesians 4:32. How should we treat others, and why should we treat them that way?

    Rebekah made a big mistake by not taking a forgiving attitude. Instead, she quickly put a plan into action. Jacob was to get a goat, and she would make the stew. Do you really think that was the first time she had made this stew? Had she spent hours learning to perfect the recipe? Isaac was no match for her; she could outwit her blind, bedridden husband. She seemed to have no fear; she felt she could pull this one off. Taking a goatskin, she covered Jacob's hands and neck.

25. What makes you think Jacob got a little nervous and needed reassurance from his mother? Read Genesis 27:11 and 12.

26. Basically Rebekah said, "Don't worry. I'll get you out of any trouble. I'll take the consequences." What happens to children whose parents take this approach to child-rearing?

Jacob may have hoped to pull off this scheme without an outright lie, but Isaac simply asked, "Who are you?" Jacob answered with a lie, which he followed with five more lies. Isaac seemed to think something was wrong. Suspense mounted as Jacob tried to finish the job before Esau got there. It was a close call: "And Jacob was yet scarce gone out from the presence of Isaac his father, that Esau his brother came in from his hunting" (Genesis 27:30).

Rebekah's manipulation had worked, or so she thought. But then she heard from her spies that Esau was going to kill Jacob as soon as their father died. Immediately she asked Isaac to send Jacob to their home country to find a bride.

27. How long did she say Jacob would be gone (Genesis 27:44)?

It turned out to be years. In fact, Rebekah never saw her favorite son again on this earth. Her scheme didn't turn out as good as she thought. Nothing more about Rebekah is recorded in the Scripture except her burial, which was in the same place as Abraham, Sarah, and Isaac (Genesis 49:31).

When we reflect on the life of Rebekah, we realize that she replaced trust in God with her own scheming. God had said Jacob was to have the blessing, and He could have made that happen without Rebekah's scheming. Rebekah was unable to trust God. Her entire family suffered as a result. May God help us learn from Rebekah as we try to make a difference in this world.

❀ ❀ ❀

Make a Difference in Your World

1. Why are honesty, integrity, trust, and truthfulness so important in one's life? one's home?

2. Unconditional love gives confidence to the receiver. Do you show unconditional love to your family members? If so, how? How could you improve? When you love others unconditionally, you are loving in the way God loved you. (Read Romans 5:8.)

3. How do lying and scheming ruin communication?

4. What problems occur when parents favor one child above another?

5. What problems result from a lack of leadership on the husband's part? How can a wife encourage her husband in leadership (particularly spiritually) without being too pushy?

6. What lessons did you learn from the life of Rebekah that can help you make a difference in your world?

Miriam: The Peril of Pride

Exodus 1:1—2:10; 15:20, 21; Numbers 12

SOMEONE ONCE SAID that the hardest instrument in the orchestra to play is second fiddle. Although Miriam was a prominent and well-respected woman in Israel, she spent most of her life playing second fiddle to her baby brother. At first she played her position well, but as time passed she struggled with it. Eventually sibling rivalry emerged. In a jealous rage, Miriam publicly dissented with her brother, who was God's appointed leader of Israel. God judged her rebellion by causing her to become a leper. She recovered, but her rebellion against Moses's authority is the incident for which she is most remembered. Miriam's life is an example of how one sin can destroy the reputation of all the good things a person has done in the past. What an awesome thought!

Miriam's parents must have done something right to have turned out three great leaders in Israel. Miriam, along with Aaron and Moses, led Israel to the Promised Land; however, none of the three entered it. No doubt Miriam had a significant impact on the nation of Israel. We can learn from the good things she did as well as from the bad. She was a woman who made a difference.

❀ ❀ ❀

Study the Scriptures

The Early Days of Miriam

Let's look at the background of the times in which Miriam lived.

1. Why were the Children of Israel in Egypt? Read Genesis 45:8–11 and 47:1.

2. How did life change for the Israelites after Joseph died? Read Exodus 1:8–14.

3. How did Pharaoh try to downsize the Israelite population? Read Exodus 1:15–22.

It was during these difficult times that Amram and Jochebed had their family. Miriam was the oldest child. She certainly had the characteristics of a firstborn child. Some years later her parents had a son named Aaron; then after three more years Moses was born. (See Exodus 7:7 to confirm the three-year age difference between Moses and Aaron.)

4. What spiritual quality did Miriam's parents have? Read Hebrews 11:23.

Miriam was old enough to see her parents' great faith. Their faith caused them to make a basket and place baby Moses in it and then in the reeds at the river's edge. Parents influence their children more than they realize. How did your parents influence you? How are you influencing your children?

5. After Moses was in the river, what was Miriam's job? Read Exodus 2:1–4.

6. How did Miriam show she was a brave, responsible sister? Read Exodus 2:5–9.

The Scripture does not say whether approaching Pharaoh's daughter and offering the services of a nurse were part of the parents' plan or if Miriam took the initiative on her own. Either way, it was an act of bravery on Miriam's part. Miriam risked her life for her brother. Her arrangement with Pharaoh's daughter enabled Moses to get his early training from his mother. Miriam's relationship with Moses was formed in his early years while he lived in his own home (Exodus 2:7–10).

7. After the rescue of baby Moses, we hear nothing more about Miriam until after the Israelites left Egypt. Use your imagination. What do you think life might have been like for

Miriam from the days of baby Moses to the time of the Exodus?

Through all of this, God spared Miriam's life. Her character was molded in the fires of adversity. As a child, she showed responsibility and leadership that developed into its fullest in adulthood. These qualities must have been nurtured during the silent period of Miriam's life. When she was a mature woman, these qualities flourished as she helped lead Israel out of Egypt. During her time in Egypt, she earned the respect of her people. She captured the limelight in a male-dominated world.

Miriam's Spiritual Leadership

8. What is Miriam called in Exodus 15:20?

9. What did she do in Exodus 15:20 and 21?

The word "prophetess" is the female form of the word "prophet." When Moses led the men in a song of deliverance, Miriam led the women in a response. She used her leadership to glorify God and draw people closer to Him.

10. What three siblings are named in the genealogy in 1 Chronicles 6:3?

11. When God brought Israel out of Egypt, whom did He send to be their leaders? Read Micah 6:4.

Miriam, as well as her brothers, was sent by God. Her occupation changed from "slave" to "freedom fighter" as she helped lead Israel. The word "sent" means "called," or "formally called." God appointed Moses as the main leader, but Miriam and Aaron were also called to be leaders in Israel. These three did not appoint themselves; God appointed them.

In spite of the fact that they lived apart for many years, these three siblings seemed very close to one another. Miriam and Aaron probably did not see Moses at all during the forty years he lived in Midian. But once reunited, they stayed together for forty years as they traveled in the wilderness.

Miriam's Downfall

12. What two attitudes often precede a spiritual failure? Read Proverbs 16:18.

Even though Miriam was a godly woman, these two attitudes crept into her life and became a spiritual snare. Repentance kept her from becoming a complete disaster, but pride and a haughty spirit certainly brought suffering and public embarrassment into her life.

13. What were Miriam and Aaron's two complaints against Moses? Read Numbers 12:1 and 2.

Miriam, who was a natural born leader, seemed to be the ringleader in the complaints. The verb for "spake" in the original language is a feminine verb, which indicates Miriam was the leader in the criticism. True, Aaron joined in with Miriam, but going along with the crowd seemed to be Aaron's style. Since Miriam was the one God punished, she was no doubt the principal one at fault.

14. What principle in Proverbs 18:12 did Miriam need to learn? What are some ways we can apply this principle to our lives?

It is not unusual for brothers and sisters to be jealous of one another. But Miriam was not only rebelling against Moses; she was rebelling against God. God had appeared to Moses in the burning bush and called him to lead Israel (Exodus 3).

15. In what spectacular way did God meet with Miriam? Read Numbers 12:4 and 5.

16. What did God do and say to show that Moses was His divinely appointed leader? Read Numbers 12:7–10.

When Miriam started attacking the spiritual leadership of Moses, she got herself into big trouble. Miriam felt she and

Aaron had as much right to lead Israel as Moses. Why should her baby brother be the only one through whom God spoke?

Even though Moses and Miriam had the same parents, they were quite different. Moses thought he was incapable of leading God's people, but God called him anyway. Miriam thought she should lead beyond what God had called her to do.

17. What did Moses say about himself, and what did God say about him? Read Exodus 4:10 and Numbers 12:3.

Now Moses had a problem! Miriam wanted more power. Perhaps she was unhappy with the choice of seventy elders to help Moses (Numbers 11:16, 17). She felt her position and power were in jeopardy. Moses did not seem to understand because he had a whole different view of things. Moses did not cling to power. He realized Israel was God's nation and the power belonged to God. He wanted what was best for God's people.

This situation reminds me of church fights. In Proverbs 6:16–19 God lists things He hates. One of the things He hates is "he that soweth discord among brethren." Seldom are church fights over doctrinal issues. Often they are over something similar to Miriam's problem. Someone wants a job that someone else has or a job that is more glamorous. Church fights cause us to forget about a lost world that is headed for an eternity without Christ. They cause us to focus on ourselves. They cause us to be concerned about how others perceive us. Worst of all, they cause us to lose our sweet fellowship with God.

18. How do you react when someone comes along who can do your job at church better than you can? As a Christian who wants the best for the body of Christ, how should you react?

It is easy to condemn Miriam for her attitude yet harbor the same attitude ourselves.

19. What attitude should we have? Read Matthew 5:44 and 46.

20. Sin always has consequences. Public sin has public consequences. Miriam's sin was definitely public. Miriam had a "root of bitterness" in her heart. What is the warning in Hebrews 12:14–16?

21. What is the connection between our hearts and our mouths? Read Matthew 12:34.

When we allow a bitter spirit to stay in our hearts, it will eventually manifest itself in our speech. This is what happened to Miriam. She gave vent to bitterness within and then proceeded to drag her brother Aaron down with her. She nursed her grievances instead of dealing with them. She used her God-given strong leadership to stir up criticism of God's appointed leader, Moses. She lost her desire to please God as well as her fear of His displeasure. Strongly and swiftly God dealt with her. Likewise, God will deal with us when we harbor pride and criticism in our hearts! May the fear of God keep us from stirring up trouble among our brothers and sisters in Christ.

22. What lesson could Miriam have learned from Proverbs 15:33?

Miriam's Punishment

23. How did God punish Miriam? Read Numbers 12:10.

When Aaron saw what happened to Miriam, he quickly changed his mind about demanding leadership. He no longer wanted equality; he became submissive to Moses (Numbers 12:11). He recognized his rebellion as sin and accepted responsibility for his sin.

24. Moses had compassion on his sister. Perhaps he remembered how she had saved his life when he was a baby. What happened next in this story of Miriam's life (Numbers 12:13–15)?

Miriam sinned publicly, and God punished her publicly. For a woman who had been held in such high respect, this public punishment had to be very embarrassing. Nothing more is said about Miriam in Scripture from this incident until she died. Miriam made a difference in Israel until sin made a difference in her.

❀ ❀ ❀

Make a Difference in Your World

1. The big lesson we learn from Miriam is that no matter what great things we have done for God in the past, it is possible to blow the future. Neither Miriam, Aaron, nor Moses entered the Promised Land. Someone made this sobering statement: "Few people run well to the end." What a good warning for each of us! Examine your own life. Are you growing spiritually? Are you becoming more Christlike? Don't rest on yesterday's victories; press on!

2. We can learn from Miriam's successes and her failures. Think about yourself. What strengths should you accentuate? What weaknesses do you need to protect against?

3. We need to watch our hearts so our mouths do not say things that would bring God's judgment. Saying the wrong things comes from a wrong heart attitude. Are you harboring things in your heart that will eventually cause you to say something that you shouldn't? Read Proverbs 4:23. This is a good "heart" verse to memorize.

4. Have you ever been overly critical? What happened? What have you learned from the life of Miriam to help you in this regard?

5. What lessons have your learned from the life of Miriam that can help you make a difference in your world?

Rahab: Shady Lady from Jericho

Joshua 2:1—6:25

THE STORY OF Rahab and the spies is a gleam of light in gross heathen darkness. We often find light where we least expect it, don't we? This story proves that even people who have lived degraded lives can be transformed by the saving grace of Jesus Christ. Rahab's simple service and womanly hospitality to the spies changed her life from despair to hope.

Rahab was a prostitute and probably also an innkeeper, so the spies were able to enter her house without suspicion. She may have been a temple prostitute and therefore not looked down on for her profession. Being an innkeeper and working with flax showed that she was an industrious lady. Rahab gladly received the spies and concealed them. They willingly accepted her help. Why did she do this? It was her faith in God. She didn't know much about God, but she recognized His hand in the miracles He had done for Israel.

Rahab's act of concealing the spies proved her faith in God, but it also placed her in danger. No woman would endanger her life for something she didn't believe in. Rahab was justified by her faith, not her works (Hebrews 11:31). Her work in saving the spies evidenced her faith. Rahab's sins were forgiven when she placed her faith in God. She became an Israelite and married

Salmon, whom many Bible scholars think was one of the two spies.

In the doomed nations, Rahab is the first person we know of to escape God's judgment. She was a brave woman. A lesser woman might have shrunk from an encounter with her foes (the spies), but she welcomed them. She made a choice to risk her life for the spies and cast her lot with God's people. In effect she told the spies the same words that her future relative spoke years later, "Thy people shall be my people, and thy God my God" (Ruth 1:16).

Rahab was a remarkable woman with unbelievable confidence in the promise made by the spies. She saw nothing wrong with the falsehood she told the king's messengers. The lie seemed to be made in true faith, demonstrating devotion to God and treason to her people.

In the end, God rewarded her faith by sparing her and her family in the battle of Jericho. He gave her a new citizenship, a noble marriage, and a royal family. Rahab was a woman who made a difference.

❀ ❀ ❀

Study the Scriptures

The Spies and Rahab

Joshua 2 begins with the record of Joshua's sending two spies to view the land of Canaan and especially to scout Jericho.

1. Where did the spies find lodging (Joshua 2:1)?

The spies crossed the Jordan River and headed strai⌐ Jericho, where they found lodging in Rahab's house. S⌐ were no hotels, some women made a living ⌐ Rahab's inn could have been called "Bed a⌐

2. Where was Rahab's house located, ⌐ choice for the spies? Read Joshua 2:1⌐

God certainly guided the spies. It was no coincidence that they entered Rahab's house. He led the men to the one person who would be favorable to them. He led them to the one person who believed the reports about God and even wanted to know more. This same God can direct your life and mine.

Rahab was different than other people in Jericho. Although you would never have known by looking at her lifestyle, Rahab had a hunger in her heart to know God. So it was not by chance but by the providence of God that the spies entered her house.

Today God brings circumstances and events into the lives of people all around us to soften them and turn them to Himself. God works in the heart of the sinner and also in the heart of the soul winner. This is not happenstance; it is completely master-minded by God. God works in the hearts and lives of people around us in various ways. He may work through sickness, marital conflict, the birth of a child, or many other ways. Do you know someone who may be experiencing the work of God in her life? Could God use you to help her?

The spies were willing to do what Joshua asked them to do. They were *available* to serve God. God wants to use our *availability* more than our *ability*. Have you ever said, "God, please use me; I'm available"?

3. What was Isaiah's response to God's call? Read Isaiah 6:8.

4. Even though Rahab knew very little about God, of what was she sure? Read Joshua 2:8 and 9.

ab's Faith

eports of God's miracles for Israel had been circulated in

Canaan for some time. Now it was evident the Israelites were about to invade. Rahab believed God would give them Jericho.

5. How had she arrived at this conclusion (Joshua 2:10)?

6. How did all the other people respond to these reports (Joshua 2:11)?

When people around you observe what God is doing in your life, do they say, "There is a God in Heaven"? Don't count on a sermon to convict people; they need to see in your life something they can't explain. What is there about you that says that the Lord is with you? What is different in your life to make others want the same God you have? Too often we look like the world, dress like the world, and even smell like the world. If we are just like the unsaved people around us, how will they see their need of a Savior? They need to see people whose lives have been transformed by the gospel of our Lord Jesus Christ.

7. What deal did Rahab make with the spies (Joshua 2:12, 13)?

Rahab had concluded that Israel's God was the true God. When she spoke of God, she used the Hebrew word for Jehovah God, not the word for her pagan gods. She had already aligned herself with the Israelites and against the king of Jericho.

Rahab's faith in God created the atmosphere in which God

could work His miracles. We, too, need simple faith to believe God and trust in Him for great things.

8. What does Matthew 17:20 say about faith and how God honors even a little bit of faith? How can you apply this verse to your life?

9. How did the spies' react to Rahab's request (Joshua 2:14)?

The spies recognized Rahab's faith and promised to protect her and her family. When we see someone else's faith in God, it encourages us to increase our faith. Be a faith encourager!

10. Recall a time when you trusted God for something and then saw Him work on your behalf.

Faith in Action
11. Read Joshua 2:18–20. What three things did Rahab need to do in order to be spared when the Israelites took Jericho?

These actions were outward conditions Rahab was to meet. The real reason she was spared was her faith in God—a faith that did not stagger at the odds of the impossible.

The spies followed Rahab's advice. They hid in the hills for three days; then they returned to Joshua (Joshua 2:22, 23).

12. How did Rahab's faith influence the spies' report to Joshua? Read Joshua 2:9 and 24.

Joshua 6 records the specific instructions on how the Israelites were to conquer Jericho. The Canaanites were frightened. They knew what God had done in the past. They did not think they could win a fight with Israel. Their hearts melted and their courage failed because they knew Israel's God was powerful.

The Israelites carried the ark of the covenant and marched around Jericho every day for six days. On the seventh day, they marched around Jericho seven times then blew the trumpets and shouted.

Can you imagine Rahab watching this procession? I wonder what went through her mind. No doubt she kept a close eye on the red cord and made sure it was visible in the window. She had to keep her family in her house, which could have been a difficult job.

In a supernatural way, the walls fell flat, and the soldiers rushed in and took the city. Only Rahab's house stood.

Why was Rahab spared? Because she chose to believe God. She believed God without any evidence to her senses. Her life was an example of the New Testament principle found in Hebrews 11:1: "Now faith is the substance of things hoped for, the evidence of things not seen."

What a lesson for us! No problems in your life are any more difficult to solve than the ones Rahab had. God has not lost His

power. He is as great today as He was in Rahab's day. What problem do you have for which you need to trust God?

13. What do the following verses tell us about Rahab?
    Joshua 6:22

    Joshua 6:25

    Matthew 1:5

Rahab's life is a beautiful picture of Christ and the believer. He rescues us from the sinful world. We should want others to be rescued too. With whom are you sharing this message of salvation?

The Rewards of Faith
14. Hebrews 11:31 gives us four distinguishing facts about Rahab. (a) What are the first two words of the verse?

    (b) What was the difference between Rahab and the rest of the Canaanites?

    (c) What label did Rahab still carry centuries later?

    (d) What deed had she done, and how did she do it?

Rahab had the distinction of being mentioned in Hebrews 11, a chapter that is often called God's Hall of Fame. Her obedience to God kept her from perishing with the rest of the people. Interestingly, she is still remembered as a harlot. God's grace can transform anyone, but some past sins carry a lifelong stigma.

15. According to James 2:25, how did Rahab's actions show that she no longer trusted her pagan gods?

Everyone needs salvation—from the king to the pauper, from the good to the bad. James 2:21–25 tells of Abraham, a good person, yet he needed salvation. It also tells of Rahab, a Gentile prostitute, who likewise needed salvation. Rahab was a woman with two strikes against her—she was a Canaanite and a prostitute. Yet her faith in God spared her and her family when all else in Jericho was destroyed.

16. Is there something in your past that haunts you? Do you still carry the stigma of past sin? How can the following verses help you or someone you know?
    Psalm 103:8–13

    Isaiah 1:18

Isaiah 43:25

Psalm 51

❀ ❀ ❀

Make a Difference in Your World

1. Are you overlooking people who need the gospel simply because you think they are unlikely candidates? Don't judge a person on appearance. Don't let a person's background or lifestyle negatively influence you. God's grace can reach anyone!

2. Ask yourself, "Is there anything about my life that the world can't explain?" Like the spies in Joshua 2, people around us should see something different because of what God has done in our lives.

3. What great things are you believing God to accomplish in your life? Can you point to things He has done in the past that give you confidence to trust Him for the future?

4. What lessons have you learned from Rahab that can help you make a difference in your world?

Deborah: Israel's Joan of Arc

Judges 4:1—5:31

DEBORAH IS AN excellent example of a woman God used as a leader. She lived in the midst of depressing circumstances. God used her to be the deliverer of His people. Her prominence as a woman judge was indeed unusual for her times. In Jewish culture a woman's usefulness and happiness usually centered around the home, but Deborah was different. She emerged as a judge in Israel and advised leaders and armies. Her story shows that God can show His power through anyone who will yield to Him.

Although Deborah was not the commander of the army, she was definitely the influence and inspiration behind it. She met danger with calmness. She was able to influence a military leader and his army. She was a rare and unusual woman for her day. Deborah's life made a difference in Biblical history and should be a challenge to each of us.

Study the Scriptures

The Career Woman

When Joshua led Israel, the people enjoyed one victory after

another. But after Joshua's death, the Israelites turned from God and sinned greatly. Because of their sin, God allowed heathen nations to force His people into servitude. Eventually the people would call upon God, and He would raise up a judge, a deliverer, who would lead the people in defeating the enemy. Things would go well for a while, then the cycle would repeat itself: sin, servitude, supplication, salvation. For many generations the people of Israel vacillated between obedience and disobedience.

1. How does Judges 17:6 describe this period of Jewish history?

After the death of judge Ehud, the people once again did evil in God's sight. God allowed the Canaanites under King Jabin and army captain Sisera to oppress the Israelites for twenty years. Then judge Deborah appeared on the scene.

2. What three things does Judges 4:4 say about Deborah?

Little is known about Deborah's background. We know she was married to Lapidoth, a name given to a strong man or strong leader. It means "flame, torch, or lamp." Deborah was a strong woman who was apparently married to a strong man. She was a leader in Israel, a judge. She was also a prophetess, a person through whom God spoke. (Today God speaks to us through the Bible.)

3. What did Deborah do (Judges 4:5)?

Her office was under the palm tree of Deborah. The Bible does not say how she prepared herself to become a leader, but she had God's stamp of approval upon her, and she magnified the office He gave her. The other national leaders and soldiers obeyed her. She was determined to defeat the nation that oppressed Israel. God used a woman, a mother in Israel, not a military man like Barak, to deliver His people. The point of the story is not Deborah's great power, but God's great power that worked through her. How about you? Are you willing to be used of God and let His power work through you?

4. How did Deborah know what to tell Barak? What did God tell her to say? Read Judges 4:6 and 7.

5. What was Barak's reply (Judges 4:8)?

We may hear Barak referred to as a coward. Undoubtedly he had some fear. Who wouldn't be afraid when facing a heavily armed army with nine hundred iron chariots (Judges 4:3)? Barak must have appreciated Deborah's leadership and wisdom, so he asked her to accompany him.

Woman at War

6. How did Deborah reply to Barak? Read Judges 4:9.

Some people like to give advice, but they excuse themselves

from action. God's work has critics who can tell you what you are doing wrong and how you should improve, but they never get into the battle for the Lord themselves. Deborah was not like that. She went to battle with Barak. Actually, Deborah and Barak complemented each other. Deborah could prophesy but not fight, and Barak could fight but not prophesy.

7. How does Judges 4:3 describe the enemy?

Nine hundred iron chariots looked awesome to the Israelites. But their secret weapon was the all-powerful God Who had destroyed the entire Egyptian army, including *their chariots.* Our problems are magnified when we focus on them; they are minimized when we focus on God. When the Israelites focused on their enemy, they were paralyzed and helpless. When Deborah inspired them to focus on God and His deliverance, they defeated their enemy. Remember 1 John 4:4— "Greater is he that is in you, than he that is in the world."

8. Who did Barak take to battle with him? Read Judges 4:10.

Deborah could not lead the army into battle, but she could inspire them. Barak was a great warrior, but not a prophet. We need all kinds of people in God's work. Both Deborah and Barak were needed for the victory. We need to appreciate the people with whom we work and associate who have God-given talents and abilities that are different from ours.

Encouraging the Troops
9. Women seem to have the inborn ability to cheer and encourage the men in their lives to accomplish difficult and

dangerous tasks. How did Deborah inspire Barak to fight? Read Judges 4:14.

10. Describe the battle (Judges 4:15, 16).

Miraculously, Barak was victorious over Sisera's army! How could a group of 10,000 men defeat a large, well-equipped army? God sent rain (Judges 5:4) that flooded the stream and valley. Sisera's iron chariots got bogged down in the mud. Evidently the horses broke away and ran (Judges 5:21, 22). The confused troops fled. The Israelites went after the enemy and slew them. Not a single Canaanite escaped. Was the victory due to the Israelites' power? Not at all! The secret is found in Judges 4:15: "And the LORD discomfited [routed] Sisera." This was God's doing!

We have a great God! No matter what problems you are facing today, God is greater. Are you willing to give your problems to God and let Him solve them? We spend too much time trying to work out our own problems and too little time seeking God's help.

11. Who is the new character we meet in Judges 4:18?

Jael and Deborah may not have known each other, but they had to be women of kindred spirits. Jael's husband, Heber, was from the Kenite family, which was at peace with Sisera's country. Sisera felt he would be safe hiding in Heber's tent. In

fact, Jael went out to meet Sisera and asked him into the tent. She covered him up. Interestingly, he asked for water, but she gave him milk. He thought she was honoring him by giving him milk. However, she knew water would merely quench his thirst, while milk would be filling and make him sleepy. While Sisera slept, Jael took a hammer and drove a tent stake through his head, killing him.

12. What happened next (Judges 4:23, 24)?

The Israelites not only saw Sisera and his superior army killed, but they also saw the defeat of the enemy who had oppressed them for twenty years. Psalm 18:3 and 46 are a good summary of this account: "I will call upon the LORD, who is worthy to be praised: so shall I be saved from mine enemies. . . . The LORD liveth; and blessed be my rock; and let the God of my salvation be exalted."

13. What is the last statement in Judges 5?

After forty years of oppression, the Israelites had twenty years of peace. Do you want peace? If so, you must let God fight your battles. You may get temporary relief from fighting your battles in your own strength, but lasting peace comes when we turn our problems over to God. What a lesson to learn from this great lady judge, Deborah!

Deborah lived in a day when Israel desperately needed leadership. God raised her up to fill this need. Probably no one in her generation expected a woman to fill this position. But God did! God can use women, ordinary women like you and me, to serve Him.

14. What words describe the person who is qualified for service in the following verses?
    1 Corinthians 4:2

    2 Timothy 2:21

    Romans 12:2

As Deborah faithfully served God among His people, God gave her a far greater task, that of bringing peace to her country. We need to faithfully serve God in the tasks He has given us to do before He trusts us with greater things.

Facing Problems

15. We all have problems. Life *is* problems—one after another. What are your nine hundred chariots of iron? What looks overwhelming to you? Maybe it is a family problem or a work-related problem or a health problem. Take time to write down what is on your heart and mind. Spend some time in prayer, asking God for His help in solving the problem or in giving you grace to endure the problem (2 Corinthians 12:9).

16. You have the option of trying to work out your problems by yourself, which will no doubt lead to turmoil. Or you can let God solve your problems by working through you and giving you peace. God's formula for peace is found in Matthew 11:28-30. (a) What does Jesus ask us to do?

(b) What will He do for us?

(c) What two things does Jesus ask us to do in verse 29?

(d) What will be the result?

17. We have learned that God can use unlikely weapons to accomplish His purpose. Our weapons are described in 2 Corinthians 10:4. (a) What are our weapons *not to* be?

(b) What are our weapons *to* be?

(c) How are we to use our weapons?

Strongholds are areas in our lives where we resist what we know God wants us to be and do. Spiritual weapons, such as Bible study, prayer, and obedience to God, can destroy such strongholds.

Only two brief chapters of Scripture are devoted to this remarkable woman, Deborah. But she was surely a woman who made a difference in the lives of the people around her.

❀ ❀ ❀

Make a Difference in Your World

1. The Bible says we are not to use carnal weapons to fight life's problems. Sometimes we want to use weapons like anger, sympathy, or pouting. We think we will *feel* better by telling our friends and getting their sympathy or by trying to get even with someone. But these are carnal weapons. God wants to use the spiritual weapon of His Word. How are you fighting life's battles—with carnal weapons or with the Sword of the Spirit, the Word of God?

2. Early in this lesson we learned about the "sin cycle." When we read Israel's history, we wonder why the people did not learn from their past that *sin pays wages*. But what about your own walk with God? Have you learned not to repeat past sins?

3. Do you need to take God's chastening more seriously? Do you fear God enough to be afraid of the consequences of sinning?

4. The person whom God uses is the one who is obedient and faithful to Him. The power God uses in our lives is not our own energy but His Spirit working through us as we yield to Him. Are you yielded to Him and allowing His power to work through you?

5. What lessons have you learned from Deborah that can help you make a difference in your world?

Naomi and Ruth: From Tears to Triumph

Ruth 1—4

THE BOOK OF RUTH opens with a famine in Israel and with Naomi and her family (her husband and two sons) on the way to Moab. Sometime after arriving in Moab, Elimelech, Naomi's husband, died. Eventually her two sons married Moabite women. Then the two sons died as well. Naomi heard that God was blessing His people back in Bethlehem, so she decided to return. Even though both daughters-in-law started out with her, only Ruth made the return; Orpah turned back.

Once in Bethlehem, the two women had to find a way to survive. In the providence of God, Ruth gleaned grain in the field of Boaz, a relative of Naomi's husband. Naomi engaged in some matchmaking, and one day Ruth and Boaz were married. This "happy ever after" ending brought happiness to both women, and it placed Ruth, a Gentile woman, into the line of Christ.

Both of these women made a difference in the lives of those around them. The lessons we learn from them will help us make a difference in the lives of the people around us.

❀ ❀ ❀

Study the Scriptures

1. The setting for this Biblical account is the days of the judges. What characterized that period of time? Read Judges 17:6.

The events of Ruth probably occurred while Gideon was judge in Israel. This places the book around chapters 6—8 in the book of Judges.

2. Where did Elimelech, Naomi, and their sons live (Ruth 1:1)?

"Bethlehem" means "house of bread." So Elimelech left the house of bread because there was no bread in order to find bread somewhere else. Whether or not he should have done this is open to debate. He should have known that both Abraham and Isaac had problems when they left Israel during times of famine. (See Genesis 12:10–20; 26:1–11.)

3. What word in Ruth 1:1 seems to indicate that Elimelech did not intend to settle in Moab?

The "side trip" to Moab lasted ten years! God's ways are higher than our ways (Isaiah 55:8, 9). Regardless of whether Elimelech should or should not have gone to Moab, his going allowed two Gentile women to marry Hebrew men.

4. Read Ruth 4:10. Whom did Ruth marry? So who was Orpah's husband (Ruth 1:2)?

Mahlon was probably the older son since his name is mentioned first in Ruth 1:2 and 1:5. I can imagine that in the evenings the family sat around the fire and told stories about "the good old days." Ruth and Orpah heard the accounts of Joshua and the spies and Rahab and the fall of Jericho. They probably heard of the patriarchs as well— Abraham, Isaac, and Jacob, along with the great leader Moses.

Somehow, Elimelech and his family made the Jewish faith very attractive to these two heathen girls. Naomi obviously loved her daughters-in-law, and their hearts were knit together by their common sorrow and loss.

5. God works through people. Whom did God use in your life to bring you to Himself?

As the three women stood together mingling their tears, Ruth could have been bitter. She could have said, "I heard your stories about how good your God is, but is this how a God of love treats His people?" But Ruth did not do that. And God used the sad circumstances to work out His plan in her life.

6. Read Proverbs 3:5 and 6. How could these verses apply to Ruth? How do they apply to you?

After the untimely deaths of Elimelech, Mahlon, and Chilion, Naomi heard that the situation in Bethlehem had improved. The famine was over, and Naomi was going home! Ruth and Orpah had to make a choice: Would they go to Israel and live with God's people, or would they return to their people? Both young women seemed to have a strong tie to Naomi; they viewed her with affection and esteem.

7. What did the young widows decide to do? Read Ruth 1:14–17.

This is the last we hear of Orpah. Ruth, on the other hand, went on to become the main character in the account.

8. Read Ruth 1:16 and 17. What did Ruth say that indicates she considered God in her decision?

In one of the most beautiful statements in Scripture, Ruth revealed her heart to Naomi. In effect she said, "I don't care about marriage. I don't care if I never get married again. I just want your God to be my God, and I'm coming with you!" We can learn from Ruth to make decisions in light of eternity, not in terms of what seems easy or convenient at the time.

9. What was the response of the townspeople to Naomi (Ruth 1:19)?

Footsore and weary, Naomi and Ruth reached Bethlehem at the time of barley harvest, the springtime. The women saw Naomi coming down the road with her Gentile daughter-in-law. They kept asking, "Can this be Naomi?" What a change! She had left with her husband and her sons, hoping for a better life in Moab. She had no doubt been a prominent woman in the community; otherwise the women would not have noticed her.

10. How did Naomi explain her situation when she returned to Bethlehem (Ruth 1:20, 21)?

Naomi had no way of knowing what God was planning to do! God was going to provide a husband for Ruth (something Naomi could not do), and He was going to provide Naomi with happiness in her old age.

11. Are you facing great difficulties? Are you suffering physically or emotionally? God has a plan for you. Read Jeremiah 29:11. How could this verse apply to Naomi and Ruth? How can it apply to you?

12. Naomi didn't have much in Bethlehem, but she did have someone. Who was that? Read Ruth 2:1.

13. What did Ruth do to help provide food for the two women (Ruth 2:2)?

14. Read Leviticus 19:9 and 23:22. What was God's law concerning harvest?

Naomi probably wondered all day long how Ruth was getting along. Naomi was happily surprised when Ruth returned home with a large amount of grain. Ruth told her everything that had happened, including the name of the man who owned the field: Boaz. The light went on for Naomi!

15. What did Naomi tell Ruth (Ruth 2:20, 22)?

16. Boaz seemed to be attracted to Ruth from the very start. Perhaps it really was "love at first sight." How do the following verses indicate that Boaz was drawn to Ruth? Ruth 2:8, 9

Ruth 2:12

Ruth 2:14

Ruth 2:15, 16

17. Naomi wanted Ruth to have a secure future, so Naomi

engaged in a little matchmaking. What did Naomi tell Ruth to do (Ruth 3:3, 4)?

Even though these actions seem strange to us, they were in no way immoral. What Naomi instructed Ruth to do was part of the custom of the day. Charles Ryrie says that "Ruth was indicating that night her desire to have Boaz, who had given every evidence of willingness to perform the duties of the kinsman-redeemer."

18. How did Boaz respond (Ruth 3:11–13)?

19. Explain the transaction that took place the next morning at the city gate (Ruth 4:1–8).

20. Describe the unusual marriage ceremony (Ruth 4:9–13).

21. How was Naomi restored to a place of honor in the community (Ruth 4:14–17)?

Obed, the infant grandson that Naomi held to her own breast, would—in the plan and providence of God—be King David's grandfather!

How true was Jeremiah 29:11 for these two women. God certainly did give them a future and a hope. He moved them from tears to triumph and used them to make a difference in their world and ours. Ruth is the other Gentile woman named in Matthew 1 through whom the Redeemer came.

Make a Difference in Your World

1. Regardless of the circumstance you are in right now, God is able to bring you through and to make your life better than it was before. Do you need to trust God today for difficulties in your life? You can pray the words of Ephesians 3:20 something like this: "God, You can do exceedingly abundantly above anything I can ask or think. Your great power works in me. I trust myself and my situation to You for Your solution."

2. Ruth and Naomi had a great mother-in-law/daughter-in-law relationship. What qualities in each woman contributed to this relationship? Are you a mother-in-law or a daughter-in-law? If your relationship isn't all that it should be, ask God to help you learn from Naomi and Ruth.

3. Ruth went with Naomi to a country different from her own. The people spoke a different language; they had different customs; they had different worship. Think about new people who come to your church, Sunday School class, or Bible study. Your religious "language," your way of worship, your music may seem totally alien to them. It takes courage for people to place themselves in such situations. How can you make it easier for visitors and for people you are trying to win to Christ?

4. Boaz is called the "kinsman redeemer." He had all the qualifications to redeem Ruth from the circumstances in which she found herself. In his role as a redeemer, Boaz is a picture of the Lord Jesus. What is our circumstance (Romans 3:10–12, 23)? Why can Jesus be our redeemer (2 Corinthians 5:21)? With what did He purchase us (1 Peter 1:18, 19)? What is the great

song of the redeemed (Revelation 5:9, 10)? Do you know for sure that you have been redeemed? If not, review God's plan of salvation on page 15; then talk with someone who can help you know for sure that you are God's child.

5. What lessons have you learned from Naomi and Ruth that will help you make a difference in your world?

Hannah: From Discouragement to Delight

1 Samuel 1:1—2:21

ANNAH WAS A WOMAN who went from discouragement to delight. We can learn important lessons from her that will help us make a difference in our world.

Hannah lived in a little town called Ramah (also known as Ramathaim-zophim). Her husband, Elkanah, was a godly man who dearly loved Hannah. It appears that Hannah should have been happy, but she wasn't. She had a huge void in her life; something was missing. Proverbs 30:15 and 16 tell us that one thing that is never satisfied is the barren womb. Hannah was barren. Like many other women, she wanted a child more than anything else.

When we first meet Hannah, she is grieving, unhappy, and focused on her barrenness. Peninnah, Elkanah's other wife, had several children, and she did not let Hannah forget it!

Hannah chose to change. She humbled herself and became broken before the Lord. God did not abandon her; He answered her prayer. Hannah was so grateful that she gave her child back to God. She sang and praised God, Who gave her not only

Samuel, but also three more sons and two daughters.

Hannah was a woman who knew how to pray. She became a mother as a direct answer to prayer. Her child was born in a time of hopelessness in Israel. The Philistines, Israel's enemy, were becoming stronger and stronger, and their army kept getting better and better. Judges ruled the nation of Israel, which meant everyone did that which was right in their own eyes (Judges 21:25). It was a dark time in Israel's history. But regardless of the conditions of her day, Hannah's desire was to have a child who would love and serve God.

We can learn from Hannah how to handle the problems we face in dealing with disappointment and hurt. We can choose to hold on to our problems and become bitter, or we can follow Hannah's lead and turn our bitterness and resentment into peace, joy, and happiness.

❀ ❀ ❀

Study the Scriptures
Hannah's Homelife
1. What does the Bible say about Hannah's husband in 1 Samuel 1:1 and 2?

2. What do we learn about Hannah's marriage in 1 Samuel 1:2 and 5?

This situation is not what God intended for marriage. Even though kings and some wealthy Jews practiced polygamy, it was not God's plan for marriage. God created one man for one

woman—not several women (Genesis 2:18–25). Since Hannah is mentioned first in the Scripture, she was probably the first wife and probably older than Peninnah. Elkanah may have married Peninnah to have children since Hannah was unable to conceive.

3. Describe Peninnah (1 Samuel 1:3–6).

Peninnah intentionally hurt Hannah. Perhaps it was because she felt Elkanah treated her unfairly and preferred Hannah. But what she did was not right. This was not a happy family! Polygamy always ruins a family.

4. Hannah was frustrated because she desperately wanted a child. Why was she unable to have one (1 Samuel 1:5, 6)?

It didn't seem right. Peninnah probably had five or six children while Hannah had none. Peninnah was inferior to Hannah in character and spiritual discernment. Her cruel jibes were agony to Hannah's gentle spirit. Since Hannah was Elkanah's favorite wife, Peninnah may have used ridicule to try to make things seem more even between the two women.

Hurting Hannah

Peninnah was wounded, offended, and hurt, so she retaliated by hurting Hannah. She was insensitive to Hannah's plight and focused on Hannah's barrenness. This tension created conflict in the home.

5. What should we do when we are mistreated? First Peter 3:9 tells us two ways to respond. What are they?

As long as Hannah held onto her hurt, she was an emotional wreck and became more and more bitter and resentful. She was the one who had been wronged (not the one who had done the wrong), yet she was the one who was suffering. Isn't it amazing how the innocent party can be the suffering party? The problems that upset us emotionally can even make us physically ill.

Some of the more difficult people in our lives may be family members—in which case, it is hard to distance ourselves from them.

How badly we have been treated is not the point. God does not focus on the offense; He focuses on our response. This is so contrary to our nature. We want to hold on to our hurts, to tell others about our hurts, to devise ways to get back at those who hurt us. But God says we are to respond with blessing.

6. Jesus taught this principle. How did He say we should respond to those who wrong us? Read Matthew 5:44.

7. What is the reward when we treat others this way? Read 1 Peter 3:9.

One thing that should set apart a Christian from the people around her is how she treats those who wrong her. The Bible does not say that if we treat a person who wrongs us with blessing that this person will become a best friend. The person may or may not change. The important thing is that we will please God and He will bless us for our obedience. What could be better than that?

8. First Peter 3:9–11 continues the theme of how we should treat

difficult people. List three things we should or should not do.

•

•

•

Returning blessing for insult results in freedom from frustration and tension. It does something else: it puts God on our side. Notice 1 Peter 3:12: "THE EYES OF THE LORD ARE OVER THE RIGHTEOUS." Obeying the Scripture brings honor to God and blessing to us. "But," you may say, "if I do not counterattack when I am wounded, how will my offender know that I have been hurt? Who will deal with my offender and take my part?" The answer is certain: God will!

What if your offender does not change? What if he or she becomes worse? Check your motives. Are you returning blessings for insults to change the other person, or are you doing it to please God? Also remember that sometimes God allows the offenses to continue in order to refine us and build our character.

Hostility to Hannah

When Hannah's family went to worship, Peninnah seemed to intensify her persecution of Hannah by goading her about her barrenness. Peninnah kept berating Hannah to try to show that God did not favor Hannah. She wanted Hannah to know she was no better than herself.

9. How did Hannah handle her problem (1 Samuel 1:6, 7)?

10. What was Hannah's focus: her problem or her God? When

you face problems in life, do you focus on your problem or on God?

11. Hannah did have things for which to be thankful. List some of them.

Hannah chose to focus on her problem, but God used that problem to get Hannah's attention. It is easy to get burdened down by the weight of our circumstances. No matter how bad things are, we need to remember to "gaze at God and glance at our circumstances."

12. What does Psalm 37:7–9 tell us about facing adversity?

Hopeful Hannah

13. Elkanah got Hannah's attention by asking her four interesting questions (1 Samuel 1:8). List them here.
   •

   •

   •

   •

God used Elkanah's questions to help Hannah change her perspective. Hannah had been looking at her problems so intently that she had forgotten about her blessings. She had overlooked some very important things. In a day when many wives were just expected to do their duty, Hannah was a wife who was dearly loved by her husband. Most important of all, Hannah had forgotten how much God loved her and how powerful He was.

Hannah must have taken her husband's counsel to heart because verse 9 says she finished eating and drinking, then stood up and went to the tabernacle where Eli the priest was sitting by the door.

14. What was the difference in Hannah's weeping in verse 7 and her weeping in verse 10?

Hannah was at a low point in her life. She was emotionally exhausted. She had finally come to realize her anguish was getting the best of her. She was not only barren physically, but she was becoming barren spiritually. By focusing on her problem, she became "bitter of soul," which means she was resentful and anxious.

At this point Hannah came to God in prayer. How can we have relief from the stresses of life? The only way I know is spelled P-R-A-Y-E-R!

Notice Hannah's prayer (1:11). As she called upon the Lord, she recognized He controlled the giving of human life. God was fully aware of her situation. If He wanted to, He could give her a son. She asked God to "look" at her situation, which meant she wanted Him to examine, or investigate, what she was going through. She was humble and submissive to God and called herself "thine handmaid," or servant. Then she showed her love and trust in God by promising that if God would give her a son,

she would give him back to God. What a wonderful lesson for mothers!

15. We use the term "my child" or "my children," but to Whom do they really belong? Who gives us our children (Psalm 127:3)?

16. What is our responsibility for the children God has loaned to us for a period of time on this earth? Read Proverbs 22:6.

17. When we first met Hannah, she was downcast and discouraged because she had no children. How did she change after she prayed (1 Samuel 1:18)?

18. When Elkanah and Hannah returned to Ramah, what happened (1 Samuel 1:19, 20)?

The Bible includes the accounts of several women who prayed for a child and had the joy of seeing God answer their prayers. However, we need to remember that it is not God's will to give a child to every woman who prays for one. Many sincere Christian women today pray for a child, and God chooses not to answer for them as He did for Hannah. For reasons known only to Him, He allows some women to remain barren. Such women move from despair to delight when they learn to trust the loving

heart of their Heavenly Father and to accept the fact that He does all things well.

19. Hannah is a good role model as a godly mother. When did she start praying for Samuel (1 Samuel 1:10, 11)?

20. What did she say when she became a mother (1 Samuel 1:27)?

21. What did Hannah do with her child (1 Samuel 1:28)?

Some parents want their children to be rich, successful, beautiful, or famous. The greater desire should be to see one's children trust Christ as Savior at an early age and then faithfully live for Him and serve Him with their lives. Hannah had the joy of knowing her son was serving God.

22. Hannah did not take Samuel to the tabernacle and then forget about him. What special thing did she do for him every year (1 Samuel 2:19)?

Each year Hannah and Elkanah went to see Samuel when they made their annual journey to the tabernacle. They no doubt spent time with him. Samuel's life was much different than the lives of Eli's sons. Samuel was godly; they were ungodly. Perhaps it was the influence of a godly mother that

kept him from caving in to peer pressure and living like Eli's sons.

23. Eli blessed Hannah and made his own request of the Lord (1 Samuel 2:20). How did God answer (1 Samuel 2:21)?

24. Notice the difference between Hannah's prayer in 1 Samuel 1:10 and 1 Samuel 2:1–10. How do these prayers reflect the change in Hannah?

The last phrase 1 Samuel 2:9 says, "For by strength shall no man prevail." When we try to live life in our own strength, we will fail. Victory comes from God. Hannah learned this important lesson. Her change in attitude certainly made a difference in her home. And through Samuel's long history as a spiritual leader in Israel, Hannah made a difference in her world.

Make a Difference in Your World

1. When we first met Hannah, she was downhearted and sad. She had a void in her life that could not be solved by human means. Perhaps this description fits you as well. What have you learned from this study that will help you move from despair to delight?

2. Hannah faced unfair criticism and ridicule from a person she could not escape. Is there such a person (or persons) in your life? How can you apply the principles of 1 Peter 3:8–12 and Matthew 5:44 in your difficult relationship?

3. Hannah is known as a woman of prayer. God wants us to

pray. It is His means of providing for His children. Sometimes James 4:2 describes us, "Ye have not, because ye ask not." Take time to evaluate your prayer life. Does prayer have the priority in your life that it should have? What changes do you need to make?

4. Hannah was grateful to God for His answer to her prayer, and she did what she had promised to do: she gave Samuel to the Lord. Hannah exemplified "an attitude of gratitude." Do you thank God for the blessing of answered prayer? You may want to start a gratitude journal or some other means of keeping track of answers to prayer and God's goodness to you.

5. What lessons have you learned from Hannah that will help you make a difference in your world?

Martha and Mary: A Matter of Priorities

Luke 10:38–42; John 11:1—12:9

WHAT COMES to your mind when you read the names "Martha" and "Mary"? Maybe the picture of Martha is an overworked, overstressed lady, and the picture of Mary is one of sweet spirituality. Let's take a closer look at these sisters.

We are introduced to Mary, Martha, and Lazarus during the last six or seven months of Jesus' earthly ministry. They lived in the village of Bethany, which was located on the eastern slope of the Mount of Olives, about two miles from Jerusalem. We feel we know these people because they were so much like us. They portray our characteristics.

Martha was probably the older sister; she seemed to have chief care of the house. Mary would not have been able to sit at Jesus' feet if Martha had not taken care of other details. Martha received Jesus and provided for His comfort. She was practical and resourceful.

Jesus did a great miracle for Martha and Mary when He raised their brother from the grave. And in an act of devotion before Jesus' own death, Mary made a great sacrifice.

As we study the lives of Martha and Mary, we will see the importance of having the right priorities in order to make a difference in our world.

Study the Scriptures
Overworked and Stressed

1. Read Luke 10:38 and 40. What is your first impression of Martha?

Martha "received" Jesus into her home. The word "received" means to "welcome" or "gladly receive." Martha loved Jesus, but she became distracted as she started to prepare the meal. In fact, she made preparing and serving this meal for Jesus her top priority. The Bible says she was "cumbered"; she was pulled in different directions at the same time. Don't you often feel this way when preparing a meal, especially a meal for guests?

2. What feelings and emotions did Martha display as she talked to Jesus (Luke 10:40)?

It almost appears Martha was rebuking Jesus. She wondered if Jesus noticed, or even cared, that she was working so hard while her sister sat and did nothing. In an outburst of frustration, this busy lady gave orders to Jesus, asking Him to *make* Mary help her. Maybe Martha had already tried to get Mary to help. Maybe she thought that if Jesus told Mary to help, Mary would not refuse.

By placing the preparation of an elaborate meal as top

priority, Martha had lost the blessing of sweet fellowship with
Jesus.

3. Read Luke 10:40–42. (a) What did Martha think would
   mean the most to Jesus?

   (b) What was Martha's criteria for determining what needed
      to be done?

   (c) What made Martha feel overworked and underappreci-
      ated?

   (d) Who was responsible to do the work Martha was left to
      do alone?

Martha placed a high priority on entertainment. She felt that
serving a good meal was the way to show her devotion to Christ.
She was obviously concerned about how things looked. Maybe
there was a degree of pride in her attitude, since fixing a
scrumptious meal for Jesus would make her look good.

Mary and Martha were both responsible to do the work.
They couldn't order pizza or get a carryout meal. But perhaps
the meal wasn't as urgent as Martha thought. Maybe spending
time with the Lord could have come first, and then a simple
meal could be served later. Martha was busy—but not in the
way God wanted her to be.

Sometimes in doing God's work we feel abandoned by other
people; we feel we are left to do the job alone. When those
thoughts come, we need to examine our hearts. Do we, like

Martha, have the wrong priorities, or have other people actually let us down?

   4. Even if people do take advantage of us, how does God expect us to act? Read Philippians 2:3 and 4.

     If we focus on the needs of others, we will not feel they have taken advantage of us. As we try to see things from others' point of view, our perspective will change.

   5. What kind of attitude does God want us to have as we do His work? Read Colossians 3:23 and 24.

     Doing our work for God's approval keeps us from having resentment, whether others join in and help us or not.

Right Intentions, Wrong Priorities
   6. Describe how Jesus responded to Martha (Luke 10:41).

     Jesus would not have done Martha a favor had He soft-pedaled His response. He told her she was worried and bothered about too many things. The word "worried" refers to a divided mind. It is like trying to look two directions at the same time. The word "bothered" refers to being disturbed by circumstances around you. Both of these words described Martha exactly.

7. What did Jesus say about Martha's sister, Mary (Luke 10:42)?

Both women made a choice. Martha chose to busy herself in the kitchen. Mary chose to sit at Jesus' feet, concentrate on what He said, and listen with a heart that was ready to obey. Mary made the best choice. It was all a matter of priorities, and in this situation, Mary's were correct; Martha's were not.

An Unbelievable Miracle

One day the brother of Mary and Martha, Lazarus, became gravely ill (John 11:1). Martha and Mary knew Jesus loved them and that He could heal Lazarus, so they sent for Him. I'm sure they expected Him to come immediately, but He didn't. He stayed where He was two more days (John 11:6). By the time Jesus and the disciples got to Bethany, Lazarus had died.

8. Who met Jesus, and how did she respond? Read John 11:20–22.

Martha was confident that if Jesus had been there, He could have healed Lazarus. But now it was too late, or so Martha thought. She looked at the situation with her practical mind.

9. How did Jesus try to redirect Martha's focus? Read John 11:23.

10. How did Martha respond (John 11:24)?

Jesus wanted Martha to think about *life*, not *death*. He let her know Lazarus would experience resurrection. Let's not be too hard on Martha. Most of us would have thought only of the resurrection at the end of the age as well. Seldom do we expect to see something as miraculous as what Martha would soon experience.

11. Explain John 11:25 and 26 in your own words.

Jesus wanted to bring Martha to a new level of trust in Him. He wanted her to see Him as the giver of life and conqueror of death.

12. How did Martha respond (John 11:27, 28)?

13. Martha told Mary Jesus had come. What was Mary's response when she saw Him (John 11:32, 33)?

Jesus was bringing Martha and Mary to a new level of faith and trust in Him. He was going to help them—but He would do so in His time.

14. Read Psalms 46:10 and 27:14. What do these verses tell us to do?

Most of us have trouble waiting on God. We want things done now. But God often makes us wait to increase our faith or to teach us a new discipline.

15. Recall a time when you had to wait for God to work. Why do you think God delayed (from your perspective), and how did this situation strengthen your faith?

16. The most obvious outcome of the miracle was that Lazarus was alive again (John 11:34–44). But what else did the miracle accomplish (John 11:40, 45)?

An Unforgettable Deed

John 12 opens with Jesus in Bethany once again. Perhaps a large group of Mary and Martha's friends were on hand to celebrate Lazarus' return to life.

17. Read John 12:2. What change do you observe in Martha?

Martha must have learned her lesson! This time she was able to provide gracious hospitality to her guests. Notice that the Lord did not rebuke her, so evidently Martha had her priorities in order on this occasion.

Mary is always seen as the more contemplative, sensitive sister. While Martha served the Lord by providing for His physical needs, Mary found a different way to honor Him.

18. Read John 12:3 and describe Mary's action.

Judas saw Mary's act as a waste of perfectly good money. The perfume could have been sold, and the money used for the poor according to Judas. (Not that the money would ever have gotten to them, however. Judas, the treasurer of the disciples, was also a thief!)

19. The world may have seen Mary's action as foolish and wasteful, but Jesus recognized the purpose behind Mary's sacrifice. What was it (John 12:7)?

Jesus brought things back into perspective. He told Mary's distracters to leave her alone. She had done a good deed that anticipated His soon-to-come death and burial. In addition, He said Mary's deed would be remembered wherever the gospel was preached (see Matthew 26:13). Mary's priorities were right!

Two sisters. Two personalities. Two different ways of ministering to the Lord. Two different sets of priorities at times. But two women whose lives were used by God to make a difference in their world.

❀ ❀ ❀

Make a Difference in Your World

1. Are you more like serving Martha or sitting Mary? Regardless of which sister you identify with, examine your priorities. Are they in line with eternal values?

2. Mary valued time with the Lord: listening to His Word, worshiping Him, seeking to obey His commands. It is easy to let the busyness of life crowd out the quiet time, the time of

personal devotions. How can you adjust your schedule if you are the mother of young children? a single career gal? a single mother with all the extra responsibilities that entails? a woman who may be caring for aged parents (your own or your husband's)? Every phase of life has its own set of circumstances. Find ways to value quiet time with Jesus.

3. Are you in a "waiting on God" time in your life and you have no idea of when or how He will act on your behalf? Memorize Psalms 46:10 and 27:14. Ask God to help you learn the lessons He has for you while you wait.

4. What lessons can you learn from the lives of Martha and Mary that will help you make a difference in your world?

Mary: "The Handmaid of the Lord"

Luke 1:26–56; 2:1–52

ITHOUT DOUBT MARY is the best-known woman in the Bible. No woman had the impact of this Jewish maiden. She is a model of the high calling and high privilege of motherhood. She was highly favored of God and blessed above women, but she was a sinner and needed to be cleansed by the atoning blood of her son, her Savior.

When Gabriel announced that God had selected Mary to be the mother of the Messiah, she answered yes with a willing and submissive heart. She called herself a handmaiden (literally, a slave) of the Lord.

Mary often pondered things in her heart, looking at them from different ways and trying to understand what God was saying. We can learn from her life, from her perplexing moments, and from her questions. She was a woman who made a difference!

Study the Scriptures

A Submissive Heart

The first promise of the Messiah is found in Genesis 3:15. God told the serpent that the Seed of the woman would bruise

Satan's head. Additional details regarding the Messiah unfolded as Old Testament revelation progressed. These promises continued until about four hundred years before Christ was born. During those four hundred years of silence, Israel waited and prayed and kept expecting the Messiah to come. It is said that every Jewish mother in Israel wondered if she would be the one to bear the Chosen One.

The first word from Heaven (following the Silent Years) came to Zacharias. Gabriel, the angel, announced that Zacharias and his wife, Elisabeth, would have a son (Luke 1:5–25). A few months later, God sent Gabriel to the town of Nazareth in Galilee.

1. What do we learn about Mary in Luke 1:27?

2. List the things the angel said about Mary (Luke 1:28, 30).
   •

   •

   •

   •

3. What did the angel say about the child she would conceive (Luke 1:31–33)?
   •

   •

•

•

•

•

4. Mary had only one question for the angel. What was it (Luke 1:34)?

5. How did the angel answer her (Luke 1:35)?

6. What was Mary's response? Read Luke 1:38.

Perhaps because Gabriel had told Mary about Elisabeth (Luke 1:36) and perhaps because Mary needed someone with whom she could talk about her own situation, Mary went to see Elisabeth.

7. What happened inside Elisabeth when she saw Mary (Luke 1:41)?

There in Elisabeth's home Mary sang her beautiful praise to the Lord (Luke 1:46–55), a portion of Scripture that is known as "The Magnificat." These verses are filled with allusions and quotations from the Old Testament Scriptures. They reveal Mary's heart and mind. She had not only a head knowledge of the Scripture, but also a heart knowledge. Mary knew the covenant promises of God. She knew she needed a Savior. She praised God for fulfilling His promises.

What kind of a man was Joseph? He was a carpenter in Nazareth. He is mentioned at the birth of Jesus and when he took Mary and Jesus to Egypt, but not again until Jesus was twelve years old. Some Bible scholars believe Joseph was quite a bit older than Mary and that he had already died before Jesus began His public ministry.

8. We learn several things about Joseph's character from these brief glimpses of him. Match the quality with the supporting Scripture passage.

    _____ Matthew 1:24, 25   (a) Not impulsive, but deliberate

    _____ Matthew 1:20–24   (b) Obedient

    _____ Matthew 1:19   (c) Teachable

    _____ Matthew 1:24   (d) Loving, merciful

    _____ Matthew 1:20   (e) Self-controlled

It was not until Mary returned from visiting her cousin Elizabeth that Joseph knew she was pregnant. It appeared she had done wrong. Since a Jewish engagement could be terminated only by divorce, Joseph decided to dissolve the engagement quietly because he had such strong feelings for Mary and also because he was such a good man. Before Joseph could do this, an angel appeared to him in a dream and told him that the Holy Spirit was the Father of Mary's child (Matthew 1:18–21). Joseph took Mary as his wife.

The Birth of Jesus
The Roman government took a census that required Joseph

and Mary to go to Bethlehem, their ancestral home, to register. Mary, who was due to give birth at anytime, made the seventy-mile trip to Bethlehem. You know the rest of the story. Because the town was crowded, the couple had to spend the night in a stable. It was there that Mary gave birth to our Savior.

9. Who were the Baby's first visitors (Luke 2:15)?

10. How did Mary respond to all that had happened (Luke 2:19)?

Think of all the things that had happened to Mary in less than one year. She had a lot to ponder! No doubt there was much she did not understand, but she had committed herself to being the handmaid of the Lord, and she was constantly learning what that meant.

Mary and Joseph followed the letter of the law in bringing up Jesus. They had Him circumcised on the eighth day after His birth (Luke 2:21), and on the fortieth day they took Him to the temple to present Him to the Lord. This occasion required a sacrifice, and the sacrifice they brought (two turtledoves or two pigeons) showed they were poor. They could not afford a lamb.

In the temple Mary and Joseph met Simeon, an old man who knew he would see the Messiah before he died (Luke 2:26).

11. What was Simeon's specific message for Mary (Luke 2:34, 35)?

The angel's prophecies to Mary had been happy and joyous. But Simeon's prediction was different. He predicted that Jesus

would be opposed and persecuted and that Mary would feel great pain as people rejected Him. Mary listened carefully; she had a teachable heart.

Mary and Joseph found housing in Bethlehem, and there they stayed during Jesus' infancy.

12. What special visitors appeared at the house one day (Matthew 2:1)?

13. How did the wise men acknowledge that this was no ordinary Child they had come to visit? Read Matthew 2:2 and 11.

Probably the same night that God warned the wise men in a dream not to return to Jerusalem, He instructed Joseph to take Mary and little Jesus to Egypt. Herod would not tolerate a threat to his throne, so he ordered the slaughter of all male babies two years and younger in the areas around Jerusalem.

The family stayed in Egypt until they heard of the death of Herod. This time they went back to the old hometown of Nazareth where they raised the child Jesus. (Think of it: Mary had a child Who never did anything wrong!) Mary had moved several times since her marriage to Joseph. She had witnessed miracles and had seen God fulfill His promises. Nothing more is recorded in Scripture until Jesus was twelve years old.

A Lost Child
14. What yearly custom did Mary and Joseph's family observe? Read Luke 2:41 and 42.

15. Describe what happened on the homeward journey (Luke 2:43–46).

16. When Jesus' parents found Him, Mary took the initiative and gave Him a motherly rebuke. What did she say, and how did Jesus respond (Luke 2:48, 49)?

Mary and Joseph were probably the only two people in the room who knew what Jesus meant when He spoke of *His Father's* business. Only they knew His divine origin.

Jesus' Earthly Ministry

Nothing more is recorded of the remaining years of Jesus' childhood, His teen years, or His early adulthood. We don't read of Mary again until Jesus' ministry had started. By then she was probably a widow in her mid-forties; her other sons probably cared for her.

Jesus, Mary, and the disciples were guests at a wedding in Cana. Sometimes weddings lasted as long as seven days. On the third day of this wedding, the family of the bride ran out of wine. Mary knew that Jesus could help.

17. What did Mary tell the servants to do? Read John 2:5.

Changing the water into wine was Jesus' first miracle, and it gave testimony to the fact that Jesus is the Son of God.

18. Sometime later Jesus was in a house in Capernaum (Matthew 12:46–50). A great crowd of people had gathered to see Him. How did Jesus respond when someone told Him that His mother and brothers (these would have been half brothers) wanted to see Him?

Jesus was not being disrespectful; rather, He was focusing on a relationship of faith and obedience, not a blood relationship. Mary was learning this was not *just* her son, but, most important, *He is God's Son and her Savior.*

Hurt and Pain

19. How did people talk about Jesus when He went back to Nazareth to minister (Mark 6:1–3)?

Imagine how Mary must have felt as the people talked about her son like this! She knew the truth concerning Him. Simeon's prophecies were being fulfilled.

Mary followed her son all the way to the cross (John 19:25). How difficult it must have been for her to see His awful suffering. Jesus was mindful of His mother, and, as the oldest son in the family, He took responsibility for her future care.

20. How did He do this? Read John 19:26 and 27.

We can only assume that Mary must have seen her son after His resurrection, but the Scriptures do not specifically record

her name. We do know that after the Ascension when the followers of Jesus were gathered in the upper room in Jerusalem, Mary and her sons were among the 120 who were there (Acts 1:12–15). Prior to this, Jesus' half brothers had not been believers. But seeing the risen Christ changed these men. They went on to become His witnesses, and one of them—James—wrote the Bible book that bears his name. What a thrill this must have been for Mary—a woman who made a difference!

Make a Difference in Your World

1. When Gabriel told Mary she was chosen to be the mother of the Messiah, she responded, "Behold the handmaid of the Lord; be it unto to me according to thy word." Are you sensitive to God's leading and direction in your life? Do you have a willing heart to follow God wherever He leads you?

2. Mary's beautiful "Magnificat" was filled with Scripture. What a challenge for us today! We need to fill our hearts and minds with God's Word. We need to teach it to our children. What plan do you have for personal Scripture memorization? If you are a mother, how do you instill the Scriptures in your children?

3. Mary's life was filled with situations where she had to learn to trust God. In what specific areas of your life do you need to trust God? Look up the word "trust" in a Bible concordance. Write some of the verses you find on 3" x 5" cards. Meditate on and memorize these verses.

4. Mary learned that what God wanted for her life was sometimes different than what she wanted and expected it to be. Do you have struggles in your life that you can't understand? What promises of God do you need to claim?

5. Until the resurrection of Jesus, Mary's sons were unbelievers. She had to trust God to change their hearts. If you are the mother of unbelieving children, don't give up! Mary's sons were adults when they believed. Be encouraged to keep praying and keep trusting.

6. What lessons did you learn from the life of Mary that will help you make a difference in your world?

LEADER'S GUIDE

Suggestions for Leaders

The effectiveness of a group Bible study usually depends on two things: (1) the leader herself and (2) the ladies' commitment to prepare beforehand and interact during the study. You cannot totally control the second factor, but you have total control over the first one. These brief suggestions will help you be an effective Bible study leader.

You will want to prepare each lesson a week in advance. During the week, read supplemental material and look for illustrations in the everyday events of your life as well as in the lives of others.

Encourage the ladies in the Bible study to complete each lesson before the meeting itself. This preparation will make the discussion more interesting. You can suggest that ladies answer two or three questions a day as part of their daily Bible reading time rather than trying to do the entire lesson at one sitting.

The physical setting in which you meet will have some bearing on the study itself. An informal circle of chairs, chairs around a table, someone's living room or family room—these types of settings encourage people to relax and participate. In addition to an informal setting, create an atmosphere in which ladies feel free to participate and be themselves.

During the discussion time, here are a few things to observe:

• Don't do all the talking. This is not designed to be a lecture.

• Encourage discussion on each question by adding ideas and questions.

• Don't discuss controversial issues that will divide the group. (Differences of opinion are healthy; divisions are not.)

• Don't allow one lady to dominate the discussion. Use statements such as these to draw others into the study: "Let's hear from someone on this side of the room" (the side opposite the dominant talker); "Let's hear from someone who has not shared yet today."

• Stay on the subject. The tendency toward tangents is always possible in a discussion. One of your responsibilities as the leader is to keep the group on track.

• Don't get bogged down on a question that interests only one person.

You may want to use the last fifteen minutes of the scheduled time for prayer. If you have a large group of ladies, divide into smaller groups for prayer. You could call this the "Share and Care Time."

If you have a morning Bible study, encourage the ladies to go out for lunch with someone else from time to time. This is a good way to get acquainted with new ladies. Occasionally you could plan a time when ladies bring their own lunches or salads to share and eat together. These things help promote fellowship and friendship in the group.

The formats that follow are suggestions only. You can plan your own format, use one of these, or adapt one of these to your needs.

2-hour Bible Study

10:00—10:15	Coffee and fellowship time
10:15—10:30	Get-acquainted time
	Have two ladies take five minutes each to tell something about themselves and their families.
	Also use this time to make announcements and, if appropriate, take an offering for the babysitters.
10:30—11:45	Bible study
	Leader guides discussion of the questions in the day's lesson.
11:45—12:00	Prayer time

2-hour Bible Study

10:00—10:45	Bible lesson
	Leader teaches a lesson on the content of the material. No discussion during this time.
10:45—11:00	Coffee and fellowship
11:00—11:45	Discussion time
	Divide into small groups with an appointed leader for each group. Discuss the questions in the day's lesson.
11:45—12:00	Prayer time

1½-hour Bible Study

10:00—10:30	Bible study
	Leader guides discussion of half the questions in the day's lesson.
10:30—10:45	Coffee and fellowship
10:45—11:15	Bible study
	Leader continues discussion of the questions in the day's lesson.
11:15—11:30	Prayer time

Answers for Leader's Use

Information inside parentheses ( ) is additional instruction for the group leader.

Lesson 1

1. It was not good for man to be alone.
2. God planned to make a helper who was meet, or suitable, for Adam.
3. He saw that each animal had a mate but that he had none.
4. To help Adam appreciate Eve more. (We tend to have greater appreciation for things that we really want but have to wait to get.)
5. God caused Adam to fall into a deep sleep. God took one of Adam's ribs, closed up the flesh where He took the rib, and made woman out of Adam's rib. God took the woman to Adam.
6. Yes.
7. They were made to reflect God (made in the image of God).

8. He blessed them.
9. He walks around like a roaring lion, seeking people to devour.
10. He cast doubt on what God said by asking a question.
11. She added "touch it."
12. Adam and Eve could eat freely from every tree except the tree of the knowledge of good and evil.
13. Submit to God and resist temptation; the Devil will flee.
14. Submitting to God helps us know what God wants us to do and gives us the desire to do it. Resisting temptation involves using our will power to keep us from doing wrong.
15. The serpent deceived Eve.
16. The lust of the flesh, the lust of the eyes, and the pride of life.
17. As God talked to the serpent and Adam and Eve, it seems Adam had been right there with her (see Genesis 3:6).
18. Their eyes were opened, and they realized they were naked. They covered themselves with fig leaves and hid from God.
19. Filthy rags.
20. By grace through faith in Jesus Christ.
21. He called for them and asked where they were. God sought them.
22. (a) Eve. (b) The serpent.

Lesson 2

1. God told Abraham to leave his country and family and go to a land God would show him.
2. God promised to make of Abraham a great nation, bless him, and make his name great. God promised to bless people who blessed Abraham and to curse people who cursed him.
3. At age seventy-five, Abraham left Haran and took Sarai (later known as Sarah) and Lot, his brother's son, and journeyed into the land of Canaan. He also took all his possessions and all the people he had acquired.
4. She made herself beautiful by placing her hope in God and by submitting to her husband.
5. To say she was his sister, not his wife.
6. It took her from the protection of her husband, and she was taken into Pharaoh's harem.
7. God plagued Pharaoh's house. Pharaoh reprimanded both Abraham and Sarah and sent them away.
8. That Abraham have a child with Hagar.
9. Egyptian.
10. Sarah was barren; Hagar was available; Sarah urged him on.
11. Personal answers.
12. God is like a father who wants to give good things to his children.
13. Hagar began to despise Sarah.
14. Go back to Sarah and submit to her.
15. He would have descendants too numerous to count.

16. Ishmael; he would be a wild man who would be against everyone, and everyone would be against him.
17. Abraham: Sarah's idea led him to commit adultery and use human means to accomplish God's will. Hagar: she had no choice in the matter, and it caused her much grief. Sarah: the idea robbed her of the privilege of bearing Abraham's first child. Ishmael: he could never be Abraham's heir. Isaac: it robbed him of being Abraham's first child.
18. Abraham and Sarah were to have a son.
19. She was eavesdropping from the door of the tent. She laughed and could hardly believe what she was hearing: that two old people would have a child.
20. "Is any thing too hard for the LORD?"
21. The man said, "Lord, I believe; help thou mine unbelief." Sarah believed, but she needed God's help in her unbelief.
22. Faith is having confidence in God even when the evidence is unseen.
23. No; without faith it is impossible to please God. It is only by faith that we can even believe that God exists and responds to mankind.
24. By faith Sarah conceived a child when she was past childbearing age. She believed God was faithful and would fulfill His promise.
25. At the first thought of having a child, Sarah laughed, thinking such a thing was *ridiculous*. After Isaac's birth, she laughed for *joy*.

Lesson 3
1. Genesis 24:15, 16—She was a close relative. She was beautiful. She was a virgin. Genesis 24:45, 46—She was a hard worker. (Watering camels is hard work because camels drink a lot of water.) She was willing to do more than she was asked to do. Genesis 24:56–58—She seemed confident and made decisions quickly. She was a brave girl. Perhaps she trusted God to take care of her.
2. He went outside in the evening when it was quiet to meditate in the fields.
3. She jumped off her camel (showing excitement) to meet Isaac; then she got herself ready for the wedding.
4. Isaac took Rebekah to his mother's tent and consummated the marriage. There is no mention of a big celebration.
5. She couldn't conceive a child.
6. They were married 20 years.
7. She was having two babies. They represented two nations and would be two great peoples. The older would serve the younger.
8. The first baby came out red and hairy. The second baby came out holding the heel of the first baby.
9. The boys grew. Esau became a skillful hunter, an outdoorsman; Jacob stayed at home.
10. Isaac loved Esau, and Rebekah loved Jacob.
11. Isaac loved the wild game Esau hunted and brought home.

12. Rebekah loved Jacob because he was home with her.
13. Isaac lied and passed his wife off for his sister just as his father had done with Sarah.
14. He feared the men would kill him so they could marry his wife.
15. Abimelech saw Isaac caressing (sporting) his wife; he wouldn't be doing this to his sister.
16. One of the men might have slept with her, thinking she was Isaac's sister. It appears they would have left her alone if they had known she was married.
17. Husbands are to love their wives as their own bodies.
18. Judith and Bashemath.
19. Hittite.
20. The marriages brought grief to Isaac and Rebekah.
21. He decided to marry a wife from the family of Ishmael, hoping this would make his parents happy.
22. She could have appealed to Isaac not to do something that was against what God had told them. She could have asked God for help, knowing she was praying in His will. She should not have taken things into her own hands.
23. (a) Unwholesome talk. (b) Helpful things that build up others and meet their needs. (c) It will benefit those who hear it (especially your family).
24. We are to be kind, compassionate, and forgiving because that is how God treats us.
25. He asked his mother what to do if his father touched him and realized that he was being tricked. Jacob feared his father would curse him instead of blessing him.
26. Children feel that they won't have to pay the consequences for their sins, so they have no fear of doing wrong.
27. A few days, or just a little while (a short time).

Lesson 4

1. A famine in the land of Canaan caused the sons of Jacob to go to Egypt in search of food. There they met their brother Joseph, whom they had sold into slavery. In the meantime, God had helped Joseph rise from slavery to second in command of Egypt. Joseph took pity on his family and moved them to Egypt.
2. A new pharaoh rose to power; he did not know Joseph. He forced the Israelites to work hard. They continued to multiply, so he made them work harder; they actually became slaves.
3. First the pharaoh tried to get the midwives to kill the baby boys. When that didn't work, he enlisted the help of all the Egyptians to kill the baby boys.
4. Faith in God caused them to hide Moses. Faith caused them to fear God more than they feared the pharaoh.
5. She was to stand at a distance to see what would happen to her baby brother.

6. She patiently waited for Pharaoh's daughter to come to the river. She watched the response of the princess to the baby before approaching her and asking if she would like Miriam to find a nurse for the baby. (Here we see the first inkling of Miriam's leadership and responsible behavior. She waited until the princess showed compassion and pity for Moses before she approached her.)

7. She would have been mistreated, perhaps beaten. She would have been expected to do more work than she was capable of doing. Being a slave, she would have had no rights or privileges. (She would have lived a life of poverty. The Egyptians were prejudiced against the Hebrews, who were treated more like property than human beings. They were forced to work long, hard hours and were punished if they did not accomplish enough work. Many Hebrews were beaten and killed.)

8. Prophetess.

9. She took a tambourine in her hand and led the women in singing and dancing.

10. Aaron, Moses, and Miriam.

11. Moses and Aaron and Miriam.

12. Pride and a haughty spirit.

13. Moses was married to an Ethiopian (Cushite) woman. Miriam believed God had not spoken through Moses alone, but also through her and Aaron. (Apparently Zipporah, Moses' first wife, had died, or he took a second wife. Some people even speculate that Zipporah was from the country of Ethiopia. On the surface, this may seem to be a legitimate concern because there was a danger that a foreign wife might turn Moses' heart away from God. But we know that *this woman* did not turn Moses' heart against God.)

14. Pride precedes a downfall; humility precedes honor. We need to be careful not to allow pride to enter our hearts and minds. We need to seek to be humble so God can honor us.

15. God had Moses, Aaron, and Miriam come out to the tabernacle of the congregation (Tent of Meeting), and He met them in a pillar of cloud. God asked Aaron and Miriam to step forward so He could specifically talk to them.

16. God told Aaron and Miriam that He talked to most prophets in visions and dreams but to Moses He spoke face-to-face. God asked why they were not afraid to criticize Moses. God departed; the cloud disappeared; Miriam then became a leper.

17. Moses said that he was not eloquent. He was not a good speaker. God said Moses was the meekest (humblest) man on earth.

18. If someone comes along who can do your job in the church better than you can do it, then let him or her do it. There is nothing disgraceful about working yourself out of a job. Ask God to give you another place of service where you can serve Him and perhaps train someone to replace you again.

19. Love and pray for those who mistreat you. If you love only people who love you, you are no different than the unsaved people around you.
20. Beware of the root of bitterness, which comes from the heart and causes trouble and defiles many.
21. What is in our hearts will eventually be revealed in our speech.
22. Fearing God gives us wisdom, and we must have humility before we receive honor from Him.
23. She became a leper.
24. Moses asked God to heal her. God healed her after she was quarantined outside the camp for seven days. Once healed, she was able to return to the camp.

Lesson 5

1. In the house of Rahab the harlot.
2. Rahab's house was on the city wall and was actually part of the city wall. It may have been high enough to give the spies a good view of the city. It provided an easy getaway. Because of Rahab's occupation, the men could enter the house without suspicion.
3. Here am I, Lord; send me.
4. She knew the Lord had given Israel the land of Canaan. She knew her people were greatly afraid of the Israelites.
5. She had heard of God's miracles in leading the Israelites across the Red Sea on dry ground and in the destruction of the Amorites. She believed God had done these things in the past and would continue to do more in the future.
6. They were afraid and lost their courage
7. She would spare their lives if they would spare her and her family.
8. Even if you have only a tiny bit of faith (as much as a mustard seed), nothing is impossible for you. (Ask volunteers to share how they have seen God work in response to faith.)
9. Our lives for your lives. If you don't tell on us, we will spare you and your family.
10. Personal answers. (Ask volunteers to share as their experiences may help increase the faith of others.)
11. (1) Tie the scarlet cord in the window that was used for the spies' escape. (2) Bring her whole family into her house and make sure no one left the house. (3) Tell no one what had happened (between her and the spies) or what had been told to her.
12. They basically quoted what Rahab had said; she had great influence on them.
13. Joshua 6:22—Joshua had the two spies bring out Rahab and her family. Joshua 6:25—Joshua spared Rahab and her family; she lived among the Israelites. Matthew 1:5—Rahab married Salmon (who was in the line of Christ). She became the mother of Boaz, who later married Ruth.

14. (a) By faith. (b) The rest of the people perished, but she was saved. (c) A harlot. (d) She received the spies in peace.
15. She lodged and hid the spies then sent them off in a different direction.
16. Psalm 103:8-13—God is gracious and merciful. He forgives and removes our sin. Isaiah 1:18—God can cleanse even the worst of sins. Isaiah 43:25—God promises to blot out and forget our sins. Psalm 51—When sin is acknowledged and confessed (even the sins of immorality and murder!), God can cleanse and restore the sinner.

Lesson 6

1. Israel had no king, so every person did that which was right in his own eyes.
2. She was a prophetess, the wife of Lapidoth, and a judge in Israel.
3. She held court to settle disputes.
4. God told her what Barak should do: go to Mount Tabor and take with him 10,000 men from the tribes of Naphtali and Zebulun. God would deliver the enemy into Barak's hand.
5. He would go if Deborah would go with him; he would not go if she didn't go.
6. Deborah said she would go but that Barak would not receive the honor of victory. That would go to a woman.
7. They were exceedingly strong with nine hundred chariots of iron. They had oppressed Israel for twenty years.
8. 10,000 men plus Deborah.
9. She said to get up and go because this is the day the Lord will give you victory over the enemy. She challenged Barak to remember that the Lord would go before him.
10. God sent confusion to Sisera's army. The men abandoned their chariots and ran. Barak pursued until the whole army was killed, "and there was not a man left."
11. Jael.
12. God subdued Jabin, and the Israelites eventually destroyed him too.
13. "And the land had rest [peace] forty years."
14. 1 Corinthians 4:2—faithful. 2 Timothy 2:21—clean, not defiled by sin. Romans 12:2—dedicated to God.
15. Personal answers.
16. (a) Come to Him. (b) Give us rest. (c) Take His yoke; learn of Him. (d) Rest (peace) for our souls.
17. (a) Our weapons should not be carnal (of this world). (b) Our weapons are to be of God's divine power. (c) To demolish strongholds.

Lesson 7

1. Every man did that which was right in his own eyes. (Point out that this philosophy is prevalent today. People don't want rules. They want to do what they want when they want.)
2. Bethlehem.

3. Sojourn.
4. Ruth married Mahlon; Orpah married Chilion.
5. Personal answers. (Ask three or four volunteers to share their answers. You might want to ask for a show of hands: Who listed a parent? a teacher? a pastor? a friend?)
6. When we acknowledge God's leadership, He will direct our way. We need to trust Him, not our own wisdom.
7. Ruth decided to go with Naomi to Bethlehem; Orpah decided to return to her own home in Moab.
8. She said that Naomi's God would be her God and Naomi's people, her people. She wanted God to deal with her if anything separated her from Naomi.
9. The whole town was stirred; the people could hardly believe it was Naomi.
10. She acknowledged that the Lord had brought her home to Bethlehem, but she no longer wanted to be called "Naomi" (meaning "pleasant"); rather, she wanted to be called "Mara" (meaning "bitter").
11. God had plans to prosper Naomi and Ruth and give them a future. God has plans for you, His child, as well. He will perfect the work He has started in you (Phil. 1:6).
12. A relative of her husband's.
13. She went out and gathered the grain that the workers deliberately left in the field for the poor.
14. Jewish harvesters were not supposed to pick a field clean. They were to leave grain on purpose for the poor and the strangers among them to pick up.
15. Naomi told Ruth she had gleaned in the field of a relative. Ruth should stay in that field and not go elsewhere.
16. Ruth 2:8, 9—He didn't want Ruth to glean anywhere else; he cared about her safety and charged the workers not to harm her. 2:12—He wanted God to bless her; he recognized her dependence on God. 2:14—He wanted her to eat at his table; he gave her some good food. 2:15, 16—He told his workers to leave additional grain for her and not to scold her.
17. Clean up, go to the threshing floor without Boaz's knowledge. After Boaz ate and lay down for the night, Ruth was to uncover his feet and lie there until he told her what to do.
18. He acknowledged that he was a relative of Elimelech's, but he knew there was a closer relative. Boaz knew that the closer relative had the first claim on Naomi's property (from her dead husband) and on Ruth.
19. Boaz summoned the men of the city, along with the closer relative, to the city gate. He explained the situation and offered to let the nearer relative buy the property and marry Ruth. The closer relative responded, "I cannot redeem it. Boaz, you buy it yourself!" The closer relative handed his sandal to Boaz, sealing the agreement.

20. In front of the elders of the city, Boaz announced that he would buy the land and take Ruth to be his wife in the memory of Mahlon. The people affirmed what they had seen and heard, and they wished the couple well. Boaz took Ruth into his home, and she became his wife.
21. The women praised God because Naomi had a grandson. They prayed that God would restore her in her old age. They recognized the great love Ruth had for Naomi.

Lesson 8

1. His name was Elkanah. He was an Ephraimite. He had two wives, Hannah and Peninnah.
2. Hannah was one of two wives, but she was Elkanah's favorite. He gave her a double portion when they went to sacrifice to God.
3. She played "second fiddle" to Hannah in Elkanah's affection. She was given half the portion that Hannah got. In order to get back at Hannah, Peninnah taunted Hannah about her childless state.
4. The Lord had closed Hannah's womb.
5. Don't pay back evil for evil or railing (insult) for railing. Do pay back evil with blessing.
6. Love your enemies; bless them that curse you; do good to those who hate you; pray for those who mistreat you.
7. We inherit a blessing.
8. Don't speak evil; refrain from deceitful speech. Turn from evil and do good. Seek peace.
9. Hannah wept and wouldn't eat.
10. Hannah focused on her problem.
11. A husband who loved her. A godly husband. A husband who provided well for her.
12. Wait on the Lord. Do not fret when others succeed and carry out wicked schemes. Don't get mad. God will cut off evil men, but those who hope in God will receive an inheritance.
13. Why are you crying? Why aren't you eating? Why are you down-hearted? Don't I mean more to you than ten sons?
14. In verse 7 Hannah was weeping because she felt sorry for herself. In verse 10 she wept as she emptied herself of self-pity and sought God's help for her problem.
15. God.
16. We are to train them in the way they should go.
17. She ate and her countenance was no longer sad.
18. She conceived, and Samuel was born.
19. Before Samuel was born.
20. For this child I prayed, and the Lord gave him to me.
21. She lent him to the Lord for as long as he lived.
22. She made a new coat and took it to him each year.
23. God gave her three more sons and two daughters.
24. 1 Samuel 1:10 reflects a time of need in Hannah's life. 1 Samuel 2:1–

10 reflects a time of joy in her life because of answered prayer.

Lesson 9

1. Martha welcomed Jesus into her home, an act that showed her love for Him. She felt responsible to prepare a nice meal for Jesus, but she thought her sister had deserted her. It seems she was an outgoing woman who voiced her complaint to Jesus rather than holding it inside.
2. Some possible answers are frustrated, dumped on, overwhelmed.
3. (a) Good food to eat. (b) Her own perspective and her own set of priorities. (c) She was working very hard on what she thought was important, and no one seemed to care or offered to help her. (d) It appears Martha was in charge, but both Mary and Martha seemed to be responsible to do the work.
4. We are not to do anything for selfish ambition. (Martha may have wanted praise for being a good cook and hostess.) We are to humbly serve others and look out for their interests.
5. He wants us to work enthusiastically, knowing that God will reward us. We should work not for praise and recognition from others, but for God's approval.
6. Since Jesus repeated her name twice, He must have dealt with her in tenderness and love. He was direct with her and went to the root of her problems.
7. Mary had made the right choice.
8. Martha met Him. She said, "If only You had been here, this would not have happened."
9. He tried to get her to think about life and the resurrection.
10. She thought her only hope of seeing Lazarus again was at the resurrection at the end of the age.
11. Jesus is the resurrection and the life. The person who believes on Him will live for all eternity even though she dies physically. The person who truly believes will never die spiritually (experience eternal separation from God).
12. Martha affirmed her belief. She showed she had no more questions by leaving to go get Mary.
13. She fell at Jesus' feet and wept, saying that Lazarus would not have died if Jesus had only come sooner. (Note that her response was the same as Martha's in John 11:21.)
14. Be still and know Who God is. Wait on God to work on our behalf.
15. Personal answers. (You may want to ask one or two ladies to share their experiences.)
16. The miracle brought glory to God, and it brought many Jews to belief in Christ.
17. Martha served the meal without any complaint.
18. Mary used very costly perfume to anoint Jesus' feet. She then wiped His feet with her hair, an act of devotion.

19. Mary's action was in preparation for His burial.

Lesson 10

1. She was a virgin; she was engaged (betrothed, "espoused") to Joseph; she was of the house of David; her name was Mary.
2. You are highly favored; the Lord is with you; you are blessed among women; you have found favor with God.
3. He would be a son; she would name Him Jesus; He would be great; He would be called the Son of the Highest; God would give Him the throne of David; His reign and kingdom would be forever.
4. How could she conceive a child since she had never had a sexual relationship with a man?
5. The Holy Spirit would come upon her; God Himself would be the Child's Father.
6. "Be it unto me," meaning, "Let it be."
7. Elisabeth's baby leaped in Elisabeth's womb when he heard Mary's voice.
8. The correct order on the blanks is e, c, d, b, a.
9. Shepherds from the fields outside Bethlehem.
10. She pondered them in her heart.
11. This child would suffer many things. People would speak falsely about Him. Mary would suffer because of what would happen to her son.
12. Wise men (magi) from the East.
13. They called Him the King of the Jews; they fell before Him in worship; they presented to Him kingly gifts.
14. They went to Jerusalem for the Feast of the Passover.
15. Mary and Joseph started back to Nazareth without realizing Jesus was not with them; they supposed He was with other relatives or friends. They went an entire day's journey before they realized He really was missing, so they returned to Jerusalem. After three days of searching (imagine how Mary felt during those days!), they found Him in the temple.
16. Mary asked, "How could You have done this to us?" Jesus replied that He must be about His Father's business.
17. Do whatever Jesus tells you to do.
18. He seemed to indicate that He did not know them, that His followers were actually His family.
19. They mocked Him, calling Him a carpenter and naming His mother and brothers. They were implying that He was just an ordinary person.
20. He asked John (the disciple Jesus loved) to care for her.